Advance Praise

"Glitter Saints is a powerful and tearjerking memoir of perseverance and resilience no matter what obstacles life may throw our way. Pearls are formed by saltwater or freshwater. This book tells the story of how Robin has continuously taken the saltiest and most bitter moments of suffering and transformed them into freshly formed pure gold and pearls of positivity. Facing challenges from birth to the present day, it would be one thing for readers to learn how she's created a life of transcendence for herself alone, but in every chapter of her life, prepare to learn how she uses her bodhisattva energy to create a world of magic, healing, and wonder for everyone she encounters along the way."

—VALERIE JUNE, GRAMMY-NOMINATED ARTIST AND SONGWRITER

"The voice in all Robin Brown touches is most remarkably authentic. A voice of a kind of sharing that the world needs. Like her clothes, her story truly comes from a deep love, an aching pain we all have of being human. To know these truths makes her creations have that much more value. If only we all knew how to share this deeply—that's when the healing begins."

—SHERILYN FENN, ACTRESS (*TWIN PEAKS, OF MICE AND MEN*)

"I felt like I was reading mythology, with Robin as our hero, finding her way through fire after fire, sifting through ashes for clues to great mysteries and then taking these things, turning them upside down and inside out, and returning them, as if by magic, into something beautiful...Glitter Saints is the story of someone who learned to stop and look around, take account, touch what was there that was very often painful to touch, find its beauty, and then grow that sight to a visionary level. In these times we can all be inspired by this story, by these insights, and by Robin's great energy that insists on seeing life as blessed with so much still to offer from the ruins."

—FROM THE FOREWORD BY PATTY GRIFFIN, GRAMMY AWARD-WINNING SINGER/SONGWRITER

"I love this sad 'n' happy book, and all the glitter that it took...Robin is my Vivienne Westwood, my Alexander McQueen."

—BETSEY JOHNSON, FASHION DESIGNER AND AUTHOR

THE CALL

This is the call.
If you hear the flower say paint me, paint it.
If your pain says write me, write it.
If your loss says survive me, survive it.
If your heart says do this because it brings you joy—lean to it.

Listen.
And do it.
Do it if it doesn't pay.
Do it if it doesn't make you famous.
Do it if you think you're not good at it.
Do it if you're not the best.
Do it even if it hurts and if you have to do it alone,
Do it so you might not feel lonely.
Do it because you must.

This is the call.
And if you need,
if these parts of you are lost in some maze of adulthood
with all its rules and trials and drawing out—
go back to your childhood.
Remember what brightness was in you.
And you will see,
it remains.
And you will see that that is the call.

No matter how small you've come to think your art or self is worth—to contribute.
And you must contribute.

And I mean this, in all its terror and beauty—
so remember it.
The time you have is already ending.
So say something.
Do not go silently.

That is the call.

—BY SAMUEL HURLEY, REPUBLISHED WITH
PERMISSION BY THE AUTHOR

AETHER BUNNY PRODUCTIONS

COPYRIGHT © 2024 MAGNOLIA PEARL LLC

GLITTER SAINTS
The Cosmic Art of Forgiveness, a Memoir

FIRST EDITION

ISBN   979-8-9897225-0-1   *Paperback*
        979-8-9897225-1-8   *Ebook*
        979-8-9897225-2-5   *Audiobook*

Glitter Saints

The Cosmic Art of Forgiveness

A Memoir

by Robin Brown
creator of Magnolia Pearl
with Jess Brasher
and Poetry by Victoria Erickson
Cover Art and hand lettering by Allison Lockett

AETHER BUNNY
PRODUCTIONS

Dedicated To
MY Glitter Saints....
PRESTON and ANNa ♡

WE SHatter tO shinE..
OnlY NATURE tELLS. TiME.
THERE'S No disco BALL
WithOut A BROKEN MiRRor.
No hourglass WithOut
mountains WORN tO SANd.
EVERY minuTE I see thE
glitter ON YouR HANds
EVeRY SHARd, EVERY GRAin.
Not FOR ONE second dO I
Forget to reflect.
not fOR oNE SecoNd
WAS YOuR suffeRING iN
VAIN.
i Love YOu BoTh
FoReVER aNd EVeR.
THankYou FOR ALL
Of iT *
I'LL MeeT YOu
at BRiGAdooN.
LOVE,
RobiNa

CONTENTS

FOREWORD BY PATTY GRIFFIN................................ XIII

INTRODUCTION: GLITTER.................................... XV

"STORIES ARE FOOD FOR THE STARVING…".................... XXIII

1. FERRIS WHEEL CRAZY QUILT 1

2. SUN FADING 15

3. STITCHED SONGBIRDS 29

"WE ARRIVE IN THIS LIFE AS CREATORS…".................. 43

4. SILVER MOON BOOTS 45

5. PAINT AND STAINS 55

6. WEAR YOUR REVOLUTION 71

"SO MUCH OF LIFE BELONGS…"............................. 83

7. PATCHING 85

8. DAYDREAMER WORKWEAR 99

9. EMBROIDERY 111

"LET YOUR LOVE BE CONTAGIOUS…"........................ 123

10. SAINTS 125

11. CIRCUS 137

12. EYES 147

"MEMORIZE ALL THAT YOU LOVE..." 157

13. RAW HEMS 159

14. HANDS 171

15. REVERSIBLE 179

"THOSE WHO HAVE NOT SWUM..." 191

16. RED HEARTS 193

17. RABBITS 201

18. LIGHT GARMENTS 213

"LET YOUR WILDNESS RIPEN..." 227

AFTERWORD: LAYERS AND LAYERS 229

POSTSCRIPT 237

ACKNOWLEDGMENTS 243

ABOUT THE AUTHORS 245

Poetry between chapters by Victoria Erickson
@victoriaericksonwriter

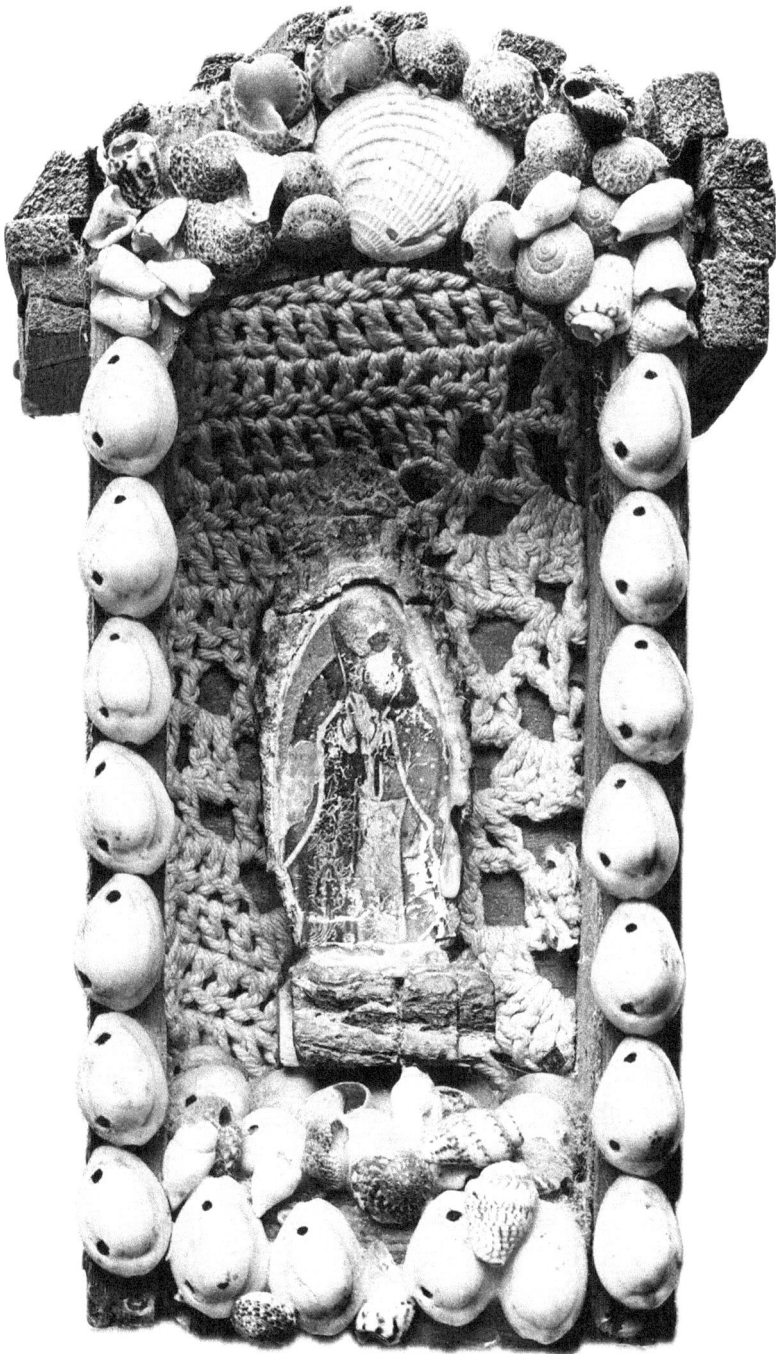

Foreword

BY PATTY GRIFFIN

AS I WRITE THIS TODAY, I'M LOOKING AT THE HANDBAG ROBIN
gave me so many years ago. These bags were among the creations that
gave birth to the Magnolia Pearl line. The bag is a patchwork of antique
brocades, velvets, fine-spun gold-lace trim, old pieces of costume jewelry,
and a remnant of a black Chinese piano shawl on the front, which has
a beautiful, many-colored, hand-embroidered bird rising from the silk.
With the help of the internet, I've identified this bird only recently as the
mythological Fènghuáng, which is sometimes referred to in the west as a
Chinese Phoenix. While I'm clearly not schooled in Fènghuáng mythology,
I still think this sacred bird is the perfect place to start when introducing
Robin's story. According to what I have read, the Fènghuáng is said to
have originated in the sun; it sometimes carries scrolls or sacred material
like the Phoenix, it is sometimes depicted with fire, and it's said only to
appear in places that are blessed in utmost peace, prosperity, and happiness.

Sometimes while reading this story, I felt like I was reading mythology, with Robin as our hero, finding her way through fire after fire, sifting
through ashes for clues to great mysteries and then taking these things,
turning them upside down and inside out, and returning them, as if by
magic, into something beautiful. Robin's is a story that shows us great

possibilities born of pain by looking for the still shining, joyful bits of things, often frayed from neglect and abuse, often abandoned, and nearly forgotten, and displaying them front and center, bathed in sunlight, loved as they are.

This kind of seeing, of finding beauty and use in what has been discarded, seems to me to be so important at this time, with landfills all over the globe climbing many stories into the sky with discarded things. Here is a story, born out of the same kind of pain that has grown these landfills—through generations of struggles, of untold pain, of lost causes, of many failures, of wanting to move on, and forgetting. Here is the story of someone who learned to stop and look around, take account, touch what was there that was very often painful to touch, find its beauty, and then grow that sight to a visionary level. In these times, we can all be inspired by this story, by these insights, and by Robin's great energy that insists on seeing life as blessed with so much still to offer from the ruins.

Introduction

GLITTER

MY PARENTS BOTH LEFT THIS PLANET COVERED IN GLITTER.
Death came for each of them right in the middle of what they were
working on. Dad had been embellishing a painting he'd done of the slain
Tejano singer Selena Quintanilla, sprinkling flourishes of brilliant red to
the roses that framed her smiling, singing, sweetheart face. My mother
had spent her last days manically besparkling an endless procession of
Halloween pumpkins, aspects of the altars that we'd set up around her
deathbed as the calendar approached the Day of the Dead.

Mom and Dad passed from this planet years apart and decades after
their explosive divorce. Both had found other loves, separate lives, and
their share of sheer-and-shit luck along the way, but neither ever strayed
from that messy, miraculous raw material that had spackled so many cracks
throughout the years.

Fuckin' glitter, man. You can't get rid of that shit.

After they died, I was permitted the gift of sitting with both of their
bodies. As I held and kissed them for the last time, patches of glitter transferred to my hands and face like tiny passed torches. For as much as the
grief burned, there was no getting around it—the light that had been on
them was now on me.

.˙.

Any time my mother came across a shattered windshield, a broken mirror, or a blood-fresh car wreck, I watched her drop to her knees to collect the shards. She'd gather these offerings in the folds of her skirt like they were relics, bring them to wherever we called home, and immediately get to gluing them to whatever shrine she was working on.

My father spent hours scouting the rubble beneath highway overpasses, kicking through discarded syringes and broken malt liquor bottles for the ideal shade of russet rocks. He'd learned to scrape these painting stones against the wide swaths of slanted concrete down there, creating large-scale murals like dystopian cave paintings that vibrated like a sunset, then faded away.

There's a story about the birth of the world that says it all began when the holy wholeness was blown to bits. Each scrap of brilliance spread and embedded into each creature, person, place, and thing in the universe, and it's only through discovering and uplifting these glimmers that we recover the world.

From childhood, both my parents were fractured by and frustrated with life. Perhaps because of this breakage, they were blessed with the gift of recognition. They saw raw material everywhere and they spent their lives elevating it. None of their creations became famous, most were never seen nor heard nor bought nor sold, but every single one of them sang survival.

.˙.

I never wanted to outshine my parents while they were alive, not that I ever even thought I could. Sometimes creativity and blood were the only things my family had in common, and both flowed generously. Asserting my expression often endangered my very right to breathe. Both my parents could be decked out like The Muppet Show Band but it was always what *I* chose to wear that was causing a fuss. All my life I've tried to figure out why, and I suppose that's the reason this book is under your nose right now.

I haven't quite figured the answer.

The day my mother died, I took home a ratty old tapestry of the last supper that she'd kept at her bedside. I clung to that thing for hours afterward. Unable to sleep, I went to the kitchen, smoothed the tapestry out on the table, and began cutting it into shapes. The only notions on hand that night were kite thread and a thick saddle needle. They'd have to do, and they did. Grounding and soaring stitches assembled the piece that built Magnolia Pearl, a humble little rucksack that bore a real true miracle.

I'm lucky the tools I reached for were those mismatched materials. How often I'd watched both my parents opt for tourniquets and syringes, can after can of Tecate, when the glitter ran out. My mother was just as skilled at finding the inherent weaponry in an object as she was at discovering where it might fit in a mosaic; my father just as apt to dash something precious to the ground as he was to nurture it. Then here would come Mom to collect the shards and make something of it.

Watching this process made something of me.

∴

The only way I survived my childhood was by protecting what I loved. It wasn't even conscious, and I can't take credit for it. My siblings looked to me like the sun coming up, and so each morning I rose even when it felt impossible.

But kids grow up and parents leave and, at some point, we find ourselves trying to figure a reason to get out of bed, a light within to reorient ourselves to. Not a product, nor a person, but a process. A practice that is a way of praying and paying attention.

When my parents died, I had a choice: I could either sink from the scars their abuses and absences had slashed into my skin and psyche, or I could uplift the glimmers. This story sheds light on it all.

In the grand scope of things, glitter may not seem like much. But in a way, it's everything: an offering, a responsibility to infinity to reflect the spark at the heart of it all. What we create from these scraps is how we heal the world, how we so love the world, and how we restore its wholeness. Hand-in-hand in this snaking parade, a human community of broken shards upon a sphere, spinning.

∴

Glitter Saints mines my life for what torn treasures exist.

I structured each chapter to communicate the chaos of my early years as I experienced them: bewildering, extreme, chaotic, traumatic, and magic.

I held onto small miracles to survive; these lifesaving methods and metaphors molded my worldview and continue to manifest through my work in Magnolia Pearl.

The conclusion of every chapter carries a takeaway thread—a meditation on how that chunk of my life wove its own particular signature and how it resonates through the clothing I make.

A poet is somebody who feels, and who expresses
    his feelings through words.
This may sound easy. It isn't.
A lot of people think or believe or know they feel—but that's
    thinking or believing or knowing; not feeling. And poetry
    is feeling—not knowing or believing or thinking.
Almost anybody can learn to think or believe or know, but not a single
    human being can be taught to feel. Why? Because whenever
    you think or you believe or you know, you're a lot of other
    people: but the moment you feel, you're nobody-but-yourself.
To be nobody-but-yourself—in a world which is doing its best, night
    and day, to make you everybody else—means to fight the hardest
    battle which any human being can fight; and never stop fighting.

—E. E. CUMMINGS

Glitter Saints

Stories are food for the starving,
medicine for the ill, courage for the afraid,
and strength for the weary.
Know your story.
Carry your story,
Understand your story.

Then sing it.

Chapter 1

FERRIS WHEEL CRAZY QUILT

I DON'T HAVE MANY CHILDHOOD PHOTOS. TOO MUCH CHAOS to capture. Same for my parents. Sometimes memory itself will have to serve and, for better or worse, it does.

I remember a lot. Trauma kept me alert. Or perhaps the peyote surging through my mother's system the day I was born propped open a door.

Mom was more prone to heroin and speed and six-packs of ice-cold Tecate; Peyote wasn't one of her standard substances. I'd like to think she'd taken it that night to connect with me; cord looped through the crown, conjoined. But I'm pretty sure she just liked drugs. Funny thing about those mescaline buttons, though—you don't get to decide what's revealed. It's more antidote than anecdote, more grounding than soaring. You get what you need.

Mom and Dad lived in a three-story old Victorian home in the Monte Vista neighborhood of San Antonio. Back then it was a neighborhood of emergent beatniks and generations of Mexican Texans, an electric mix of Virgin Mary statues and fringe from hair to hems. Their place was falling-apart-charming and huge. Different families occupied the various floors;

my parents rented the teeny attic up top, a love nest perch filled with nail polish and paint brushes, ashtrays, and tapestries. That late September night of 1963, they'd invited people up for a little party, an attic gathering lookout for those who'd consumed that sacred cactus.

Freewheelin' Bob Dylan reverberated from the record player through a sea of smoke and opiates, penetrating the walls of Mom's tight belly and finding my hearing inside her hopped-up womb. Straight from her brain to my belly button, the earthy mineral dialed open each one of my eyes, and it was time.

∴

The doctors had said to expect me on my father's birthday in November. But they say we make plans and God laughs, and I think that laughter is the most powerful hallucinogen known: the unknown. Even those who set out to seeking can't be prepared for what they'll find.

That night God laughed through me, I suppose.

The story goes that my little foot stamped out of Mom's body right there in that attic, tethering all those revelers' trips to the flesh-and-blood immediate world. It was fight or flight for me from the get-go—no snooze button on a smoke alarm. *Get up baby, you gotta get out of here!* I was jumping from a burning building that never stopped burning.

Thank God there was a hospital close by. I was a quick one: two months early and three pounds heavy, born breech, with the cord around my neck. My dad's galaxy eyes were the first things I saw on this Earth. No better witness than that. I was so much his twin I have to think we recognized each other and laughed. Found and forever bewildered.

Dad's stoned laughter startled my tiny limbs awake and tied me to delight. He said my eyes were alert from the first, eager pinpoints ready to tick off boxes and cut through all the bullshit at a clip. I was here to do a job, get this cycle of the circus started. He held me tight for a minute, our twin visages reflecting God back to each other, and then they popped me straight into the incubator like a little potato.

I was a wrinkled-pink creature gasping for air, a baby astronaut: Earth-side but not quite. Hooked on heroin and more, at least. My first duty was to detox; my first lesson was breath.

We are born perfect, whole, and immediately in need.

Taking a breath is no choice.

Is any of it?

∴

Besides my father's watchful blue orbs, made wavy and otherworldly by the thick plexiglass of the incubator, fabric was my first consistent contact. I cocooned in there for a few months, my miniature fingers bumping the rubber tubing that ran to and from my form, grazing nubby cotton hospital blankets, developing connections, and delineating my place in space based on feel. My skin drank in what my lungs and tummy couldn't. It was my first language, my mother tongue—tactile, animate, and entire.

Across the room from my little universe, my mother orbited in her turmoil, detoxing from the same opiates that surged through my small system. Our matched dependence mirrored something much larger: within the incubator, I felt around in my need, but from Mom's vantage, all she could see was her own reflected back. Her petrified-wood eyes bore holes into the back of my father, who couldn't stop looking at me. Mom turned her face away and didn't meet my eyes again for decades.

Get me safe beneath my father's gaze.

"Failure to thrive" was what the doctors said, not a disease but a condition: you *aren't* getting what you need. Dad sensed we could lick it and took it as a dare. When he was told I likely wouldn't survive, he asked if he could take me home to die in nature, with the sun on my face, beneath the fig tree in the backyard.

I left the hospital cradled in the crook of his arm. He placed me on his lap beneath the steering wheel, petting my little head and teensy feet the whole way home. By the time we arrived, that warm rhythm had awoken something within me. With each stroke upon my soles, a steady breath filled my lungs.

Good thing for methamphetamines. Those suckers kept Dad alert for nearly two straight weeks, just rubbing my feet. I ripened with each little pat at the foot of that storied fig—expanding, filling, settling into this skin suit. Eureka, a triumph.

Beep beep, little baby, you're clear to launch.

⁘

I'm surprised my mom had kept me at all. By the time she delivered me at twenty-six years old, she'd already had two babies, raised to toddlerhood, then surrendered to an orphanage. They were the output of her marriage to a nameless, faceless, nice-enough guy whom she divorced soon after handing the babies over.

Women make the choices they must, and sometimes they cut. Sewing pieces of aether to flesh was the gut root of my mother's creativity—her womb already slashed with blood-red glyphs, her battleground body that, despite it all, insisted on making something beautiful from a place of such pain. Anna Louise, my mother. A shabby pattern and a flank full of arrows. Sharp shears and deep darkness.

Anna was born in June of 1937 in San Antonio, Texas, to her mother Louise, an antiques dealer, and her father Porter, a dyed-in-the-wool carnie who owned his own Ferris wheel. When the marriage went sour, Porter rolled off with the carnival. Louise told young Anna her father had died. So it goes.

As far as Louise was concerned, if things weren't spoken, then they hadn't happened. My grandmother filled silences with her own fictions, which were the final word. She was never generous about the day-to-day details of my mother's childhood, and Anna, as well, stayed quiet.

Mom's only saving grace was a nascent creativity that never stopped. And even this life-saving God-sent gift was only ever mentioned in a cast-aside way. *She would draw*, my grandmother shrugged when I asked. Draw she did, but tossed-out talismans and textiles were Anna's true realm. The alchemy of fabric transmitted its chemistry to my mother as she toddled through towering stacks of garments Louise collected for her antiques trade: dusty piano shawls, moth-eaten silk curtains, stiff christening gowns, and stained

Victorian nightshirts embroidered with the initials of the long-passed. The wealth within what's so often overlooked was revealed to my mother in these moments, as she hid from her own mother. Salvaging became Anna's savior, transforming all she was afraid to feel upon found objects.

⁘

Louise beat Anna down every chance she got—physical and verbal assaults that cracked like lightning without warning. Mom was a pest; then she became prey.

When my mother was six years old, Louise remarried. Bill was military-razor-clean and a stereotypical "Good Man" in those times, but behind closed doors, he was pure evil incarnate. In all the ways you can break a person, Bill tried to break Anna. And in all the ways we define "wholeness," he seemed to have succeeded.

Mom's body became Bill's property. For six relentless years, Bill brutally molested my mother. After each assault, he would lock her away in the attic or a closet where she was kept in total darkness for hours or even days. The whole time, Louise knew. She knew what was going on, and she didn't do a damn thing except, every so often, send her daughter away to her grandmother Peggy.

Peggy was an old homesteader, a pioneer woman with Swedish roots who grew orchards of fruit trees and tended neat herb and vegetable gardens. She made and mended every textile in her home and sprinkled them with lavender water distilled from her fields. Louise occasionally dropped my mother off at Peggy's before rushing back to Bill. Anna would gather up her battered body, wander into this sweet, warm Shangri-La, and instantly collapse beneath quilts compiled from her ancestors' dress scraps.

⁘

As Anna rested beneath these remnants, cradled in the integrity of these hand-sewn works, her subconscious arranged itself into its own pattern of protection.

Every single one of us starts life as bits of possibility, scattered pieces of personality. Each of these identities plays its role in the psyche from inner child to chimera, and as we grow, they usually gel into a single lens of consciousness—a more-or-less cohesive sense of self.

But when a child experiences consistent inescapable torture, especially sexual in nature, as Anna did, those identities stay separate. My mother would be in her early fifties by the time we learned its name, but Dissociative Identity Disorder (or "DID," once known as Multiple Personality Disorder) evades description at any age. The personalities, or "alters" as they are called, stay with the individual throughout their lifespan as vigilant protectors, paradoxical and primordial—a motley choir of angels singing off-key and out of time the same hymn. They're that spirit's tenacious attempt to stay vital, and they stick around to the end.

It's not a failure of the mind, but an absolute fucking triumph. Creativity isn't something we choose—it's how we're made. And how we survive.

∴

But at the time, nobody knew this. And nobody except Peggy gave a shit about any of it.

She'd read the language of abuse upon Anna—bruises and winces, silences and easy startles—but Peggy never pressed my mother about it. She just fed her and let her rest. When Louise got pregnant by Bill and a new baby sister arrived, Peggy had a reason to drop by unannounced. What she found was the infant alone in her crib, starving and soiled, and my mother locked away in the attic, just skin and bones.

Peggy served some old-school justice and got Bill banned from the state of Texas, but there wasn't enough open space or lavender-scented handmade quilts to soothe my mother after all that.

From a young age, between naps at Grandma Peggy's, Anna began tiptoeing through the bright, warm kitchen to the familiar darkness of the pantry, drawn to a stash of vanilla extract. She downed bottle after bottle. That hint of numbness Mom required to even conceive of hope in the light-starved dim where she believed she belonged—she'd never stop seeking that release. At age eleven, cigarettes helped her through the long days of raising her little sister. Snuck beers with friends escalated to weekend-long pill binges. By the time my mother was fourteen, she was fully in the scene, hardly ever in school, and almost never sober. At sixteen, she started heroin. She was a rocket that could never get high enough or go fast enough, spinning and seeking a safe place, a single light within. Until the day she died, none of us dared outshine what glimmer she could muster. We flocked to it like moths at the smallest suggestion of warmth.

∴

If you were on the fringe in any way in San Antonio, on the cusp of the 1960s, Worthy Wolf was your guy. A dude straight out of a Larry McMurtry novel, Worthy was a Texan unlike any other: a fabulous art and antiques collector, rich as a sultan—an out gay man in a time when to exist as such was pretty much illegal. He threw extravagant parties at his huge home, packed with pretty girls and boys, curiosities, collectibles, and lots of drugs. Loud music and even louder fashion lured my mother to that palace of excess. She was fourteen, enthralled by all she saw and all she could consume. Across her path wandered a cute young man about her same age, smarter and sweeter than anyone she'd ever met: my father, Preston Brown. By virtue of their being the youngest ones there, they hit it off—bold and high out of their minds, but still so young and awkward. They hung out and shared a smoke, but that was it for then—the first little transit for these two planets.

In America, even the freest of thinkers felt pressured to conform. The notion of life as an unfolding journey was for communists and lazybones. Hippies hadn't even invented themselves yet, and the beat generation just drove speedy-straight through Texas. There wasn't a movement close enough for my parents to align with, so as they parted after Worthy Wolf's party, they followed the map society had laid out for them, cursing every turn.

Anna and Preston crammed the whole of their individual programming into a few short years. Even as she dabbled with heroin, my mom continued to raise her baby sister. When some OK-seeming guy came along, Anna just up and married him. She had those two babies until she didn't; then she got a divorce. All by age twenty. My father also found someone OK to marry and then joined the Navy for four years. He watched the first nuclear bomb test at Bikini Atoll, and it shook him, but he stayed in service. He traveled across Japan and Asia, returned home, and got his own divorce.

Dad

As my parents were off living and dying to these roles that just weren't right, Worthy Wolf rolled right on. Both newly free and still such babies, Preston, and Anna attended another of Worthy's never-ending parties. This time, they clicked—a cataclysm, a catalyst—the Big Bang and the nuclear bomb all in one.

∴

With the straightjacket of what was expected of them so recently wriggled off, my parents set out to sparkle—their revolution would be told through shimmer, sheen, and shellac. Throwing glitter in the eyes of the bear of society, prettying up the powers that be. They joined beauty school together: Mom did nails, and Dad did hair. "Mr. Preston" was one of the first to use a straight razor instead of shears, and this technique put him on the edge of real acclaim. He and Mom shared space in a funky beauty salon in Alamo Heights, as counterculture as you could get in Central Texas without getting arrested.

They expanded consciousness and pushed boundaries with the paraphernalia to boot: polish and razors, needles and vials. Side by side and in cahoots, they took on the world. Joined at the hip and by the vein, junkies early on. And then Mom got pregnant with me.

She was detached from the quickening. My forming flutter kicks didn't move Anna in any nurturing direction. She just kept on doing as she did; nail polish remover was the least of my worries. It permeated through the placenta, all of it, substances, and scorn.

I guess Mom ultimately had me for my father. Where she wanted a scapegoat, he craved a companion, the imaginary friend his only-child heart had longed for.

My tiny fuzzy body slipped right into the space in his life that'd been carved out by a duckling. At the age of nine, Dad had discovered this fuzzy yellow creature clumsily following its momma on the banks of the Medina River. This riverside was Dad's playground and perch, his holy place where he knew every tree and boulder. He thought the duckling was so cute—scooped it right from its waddle and put it in his pocket.

He was gonna be its daddy, and that night, he snuggled the creature into his pillow to keep it warm. By morning, the poor thing had smothered to death. He buried it and confessed all to his mother, clinging to her skirts and crying and crying.

He carried that innocent grief with him forever.

⁂

My father spent a lot of time close to the ground. Withstanding his particular childhood required it: solitude in nature among creatures like him, small and out of the way.

His wasn't the worst scenario, growing up alone smack in the middle of the Texas Hill Country. He'd been born 1,500 miles away, though, in Brooklyn, to a mother hard of hearing and forever young at heart. My paternal grandmother Helena had traveled to America from Poland as an infant on a big ship welcomed into Lady Liberty's harbor. Along the way, a scourge of diphtheria had run rampant upon the vessel, taking Helena's hearing and the life of her twin sister, buried at sea.

The disease had frustrated the formation of certain regions of my grandmother's mind, keeping her in permanent innocence. She looked at the world forever through the lens of a child, and she reflected what she saw in her drawings: dreamy, intricate rosettes, perfectly shaded wolves, and songbirds in flight. Brooklyn then had more snatches of feral landscape, patches of wetlands, towering trees, and grasses full of woodland creatures finding their way. How it all flowed and flourished coursed through Helena's sight, sharpened through her hearing loss, and imparted through her pen.

At a very young age, Helena worked in a dress factory. Her deft little fingers spun handmade lace, and she could tailor a garment to fit like a glove. The movement she understood in nature swirled into sketches of dresses. By age fourteen, she'd become a master patternmaker. This new status brought her hearing loss to attention, and the factory boss fitted her with primitive hearing aids. She learned to speak, and she could now hear those songbirds she'd drawn. It was a whole new facet, lush and beautiful, but boy, then she had a baby.

My grandfather, Preston Sr., was a pious, hardworking man. He was a stonemason, an engineer with a feel for solidity and an eye for foundations. By nature, he was a lot like his materials: stable, silent, and somewhat cold. Once they married and Helena became pregnant with my father, Preston Sr. decided a change of scenery would serve his growing family well. He'd heard that Texas had the oldest Polish settlements and churches in all of North America, so after my father, Preston Jr., was born in 1937, they moved to the teeny town of Quihi, Texas.

Quihi was the polar opposite of Brooklyn. There was no bustling community or humming machines. In all the vast and sudden, solitary silence of backwoods Central Texas, my grandmother sat suspended, overwhelmed by isolation—so much like a child herself in so many ways—with a baby at her breast. Here-and-there weekends whirling through the local dancehall with Preston Sr. weren't enough. Eventually, the small family traveled up the creeks of the Medina River to the bigger city of Bandera, but even there, Helena's only company was my young father. If my grandfather was home at all, he was reading, studying, working. Aloof, or otherwise, just away.

Though she tried to stay busy drawing or sewing or teaching swimming lessons to children in the Medina, Helena couldn't manage the crushing seclusion. She started drinking wine, lots of it. Her childlike sweetness turned on a dime, as it does, to nasty tantrums. My father bore the brunt.

Before he was mobile, Dad would just loll about alone as Helena wept and raged and slept. Once he could manage a bit on his own, my dad cleaned his mother up when she got sick and wiped her endless stream of tears. Helena swatted and swore at Preston in her desperation, then passed out for many hours. Dad would get her all tucked in, then slip out the back door to disappear into nature—foraging and resting, floating beneath the giant cottonwoods on the Medina. Drawn to the roots and devoted to the cycles, my father found all the safety, supplies, and guides he sought: handfuls of ochre rocks, berries, sticks, and tender creatures. The value of paying attention, the benefits of a quiet mind.

A dude ranch along the river recruited him for work, and Dad took to it. Hard hours spent breaking horses and clearing brush earned him time in the sunshine, always with a dip in the river at the end of the day. That pure sense of duty balanced with wonder was the underlying equilibrium he sought to recapture his whole life.

∴

Around the time she'd turned fifteen, my mom learned her father was actually still very much alive. She'd sought him out that year when the carnival came through San Antonio during the city's annual Fiesta time. Porter Click was standing right at the foot of his Ferris wheel like he'd been waiting for her all along. In a heartbeat, father and daughter jived, birds of a feather. Mom had that carnie spirit and wanted to run away with the circus, too—the whole smoke-and-mirrors master illusion.

But by the time I was born and my little bunny body was breathing strong, she and my father decided to move to California instead. The pull of the movement—music, drugs, art, and a community of like-minded freaky people opening their minds and asserting their truths, getting naked, and singing their hearts out—was too much to pass up. The circus of the 1960s embodied a psychedelic reality whose spirit radiated from the central hub of the Sunshine State.

Before heading west, we three dipped south to Poteet, Texas, so Anna could bid her father farewell. Porter and a friend had started up the Poteet Strawberry Festival in the 1940s, and he'd rolled his wheel there that spring of 1964. I was just a few months old, a scrawny, scrappy, wiggling thing in a fat cloth diaper and thrift-store coveralls. Porter's rough mitts cradled me like a catch of forest fruit as I cooed and drooled, reaching for that shiny wheel.

Soon as Mom and Dad stepped away for a second, my grandfather carted me to the tip-top of his wheel, clenching me under one arm and holding a big wrench in the other, a lit cigarette dangling from his lips. He'd eyed something up there that needed fixing, and it was nothing to shuffle me up with him. The wheel was just a typical part of his terrain, its spin familiar.

From incubator to Ferris wheel in a few short months, all carnie blood and blessed inspiration, I was headed West. My Texas send-off was at the helm of a festival celebrating ripe, rocket-red berries, rising.

Of course, I couldn't see all the way to California and everything that was to come from way up there. Even if I had, I think I still would've wanted to come back down to Earth—to keep on going with those two little figures, my father and mother, who appeared to me from up there as dots, as far away as stars and made of the same stuff.

∴

Maybe at the end of our lives, we get a Ferris-wheel vantage of the whole tapestry; the quilt laid flat, answering for its complexity. At the beginning, we're handed frayed and stained flowery bedsheets, a scrap of polka dots, a snatch of strawberry print. Tattered as they are, there's a sustaining sweetness.

The oldest pioneer quilts conceal bits of paper batting between their threadbare layers: postcards, recipes, clipped snippets of newspaper poetry. Every spare material had a part to play: fragments of experience and feeling arranged in a repeating pattern, little sewn sound bytes spinning ordered fractals. Or, perhaps the pattern is no pattern at all, a "crazy quilt" of abstract shapes that seem to defy order.

Both methods follow nature; all are part of a whole.

The women (and they were usually women) who made these quilts did so as part of their survival, which is in itself a hope. Hope for something beautiful and useful and triumphant and lasting to come from suffering. A longed-for little child who will take the scraps and craft something the world has never seen.

You're here, which means somebody loves you, which means you deserve to be loved.

The things God creates aren't junk.

Chapter 2

SUN FADING

THEY SAY IN EVERYONE'S CHILDHOOD, NO MATTER HOW
wretched, for at least one moment, we experience something simple and
bright that fastens us to our inner divinity: we're handed the sun and find
it familiar. It's a common theme in fairy tales—magical golden balls rolling
into the scene, summoning. In normal life, it can be a little more subtle: an
afternoon spent on the grass staring up at the clouds or watching a ladybug
maneuver the valleys of your palm. Whatever shining example creation
presents, we absorb its radiance like a luminous orb held harmonious in
our hearts, burning stronger than all the bullshit from that moment 'til
forever, eternally urging us to remember.

For me, that golden ball was the California sun.

California in the '60s was like a psychedelic trip, even when you weren't
tripping. The whole atmosphere was bursting with *becoming*. Anti-war
protests, love-ins and be-ins, civil rights and drug wars, urgent music and
mystics all swept up like the sublime Santa Ana winds, aswirl as the planet.
And everyone there, from hippies to housewives, detected it like animals
before a storm.

It was sewn into what people wore—it was all like walking art. People
either dyed it by hand or stitched it by hand, and you were just surrounded

with that. It was the nature of things. Taking up space and reclaiming power meant taking things into your hand, even if it was just a needle and thread or a bucket of dye. Your soul on your sleeve.

∴

For the most populous state in the country, for all its traffic and sprawl, you never forget, in California, that you are living on a Capital-P Planet. Elemental Earth urges all around you with the force of an unashamed woman. Worn scars and wildfires, vast oceans, and deserts, fresh fissures, and the feeling that, at any moment, her mood might shift.

And it might.

And the light. God, the light.

Better writers than I have tried to describe California's light. Like explaining the wind to a child. You have to see it and feel it to realize it, but you will never grasp it.

A blanket of sun pinking up my cheeks, playful wind tumbling knots in my unruly toddler hair—days of riding with my dad on his blue Triumph motorcycle imprinted my soul. From laying in his lap behind the steering wheel as a struggling infant, to propped on the gas tank before him as a small child, I'd gone from fighting for breath to finding laughter. My dirty little fingernails dug into his tanned forearms as they draped over the chrome handlebars.

In those days, nothing was childproof.

This was before helmet laws, probably before they even *made* helmets for children. I usually didn't even wear shoes on these rides. If the gas tank got too hot, Dad just pulled over and put his jean jacket under my butt, and off we'd go!

I thought we were fuckin' Helios himself pulling the sun across the sky on our Triumph chariot. Rubber hugging the road, Dad and I holding onto each other. Wind-whipped dry smiles and tears in the corners of our eyes. On the way to or from some poetry reading or meeting of musical minds, our shared adventures. The ridges and turns of Hollywood and Malibu, Topanga Canyon, the PCH: that first glimpse of the Pacific as we rose upon a hill like a great inhalation, like flying or falling in love. Leaping off the bike into the sand and scrambling out on rocks and jetties, picking up shells and crouching down to watch the starfish cling.

We'd bring worn sea glass back home in our sandy pockets and tie them with string to bits of driftwood, makeshift chimes whose notes mark time. Sitting at our dinky coffee table, our bounty spread before us, aquamarine and emerald-green shapes tumbled smooth; Preston would guide my hands in forming firm knots, clear and patient instructions as though he was teaching me surgery. It was the same serious tone he'd used at the very same table as I balanced between his knees watching him cook up heroin. I can still hear his voice explaining each article in the process, the stages of how to shoot up safely, and what to do if he didn't wake up.

He'd shown me how to take a small mirror to his nostrils to ensure he was still breathing. I did it more than once. On those dragged-out days, our sea-glass chimes soothed me like waves, assuring the sun would peek through the clouds of my lonesome once more. They were the background noise as I rode tight circles around our tiny square patio, the accompaniment to my percussion as I nailed scrap wood together for a dreamed-of treehouse. Once my father roused, he'd shoot up again, and upon the Triumph, we'd set out, both high-as-kites happy.

Of course, none of it was "safe" by any typical standards, but I never felt safer than when I was on that bike, body and soul. Safe is a relative term. The sun itself can burn you, but it's nice and necessary to bask in its warmth. We are always in peril; we just gotta find what it is we're willing to risk it all for.

∴

For Preston at that time, safety was secondary: it was all about the score.

Dad wanted to get to the heart of everything. Any membrane that separated him from experience had to be breached. That's why he rode the bike; he needed that direct immersion. And it's why drugs were so alluring to him at first.

There were about six hundred safes in Los Angeles pharmacies then, and he hit up a good portion.

Easter 1967, the first dress I made.

Pills were portals and backstage passes, the heartbeat of song lyrics and the baseline to stay up singing 'em. It was easy enough to get a script, but how much fun was that? No match for the thrill of slithering through ceiling ducts and lowering yourself into pharmacy back rooms like some trickster cartoon. Preston's seashell ear to that cold metal box. *Click click click DONK!* A lock's slight lisp, a slip-up, just enough to decipher a pattern.

In his stint in the Navy, before he met my mom, Dad excelled in the art of Morse Code: the transmission and reception of dots and dashes and dead air, a sequence of symbols. Ear-to-fingertip and back, a vibrating filament that throbbed inside of Preston always, a hyper-perception honed by Uncle Sam.

The safe-cracking gig was fun, and he had a good run. He never got busted, but eventually, his stash got slight, and he wanted to find a way to re-up that allowed me to come along for the ride.

∴

Every endeavor has its own particular poetry. The vocabulary of the hair game fits right into the narrative: fringe, fur, shock, locks. Preston loved it, and he was good at it too. Real good. And in demand. He was the IT guy in town who gave the most sought-after shag cut, like Edward Scissorhands, decades before the film took shape. The fact that he was handsome and hard to find only helped. We didn't have a phone at our house, so our neighbor served as switchboard and front desk, yelling over the fence whenever someone called.

Dad took me along to these cuts to have some motherly company: Hollywood Hills housewives, hopped up and zoned out, smoking and seeking, coral lipstick and faraway eyes. They fed me and gave me the run of their sprawling homes as they sat in the kitchen with a towel around their neck, confessing all to my father.

His sharp eye caught onto the access they granted me. Preston knew these women were being prescribed a buffet of pills, legitimate scripts from the same safes he'd once stiffed. He could practically see through

the maid-scrubbed medicine cabinets, all those translucent orange vials
lined up like looking-glass versions of Emerald City. And he had just the
little girl to get him past those gates.

A kid is a key.

And an addict's an addict.

Like Addie and Mose in *Paper Moon,* Dad and I became a little duo.
We'd roll up on the purring Triumph, one little tumbleweed ragamuffin
and her handsome Papa: a slick tongue and quick snippin' fingers. I was a
walking *Physician's Desk Reference* by five years old, able to eye the tablets
and tinctures Dad favored by shape, color, and glyph. Narcotic alphabet
lessons: "C" for Codeine, "P" for Paregoric.

*Kid, at some point, ask to use the bathroom. After you flush, turn on the
water and open the bottom drawer below the sink. Climb up on it to reach the
medicine cabinet. COUGH! COUGH! when you open it in case it squeaks!
Get the pills out of the bottles and stick 'em in your sock. Close the cabinet and
the drawer, and don't forget to turn the water off. Then come out and give me
a wink if you got what we need.*

We.

Not all drugs are ingestible.

I got just as tangible a high from Dad's involving me in his kaleido-
scopic quests as he did from those pills. I was a natural at the game because
I loved it. I loved him. I knew that things were just more fun and Dad was
happier when he had his "medicine." It was all drawn shades and shivering
under thick blankets when they ran out. My bones ached for the sunshine
and his smile, which were one and the same to me. Dad was addicted to
drugs, and I was addicted to him, pure and simple.

Staring at the sun burns blind spots in your perception—places you
can't see, wormholes where intentions and explanations interweave. In
these spaces, there was sewn within me a premature sense of responsibility.
My Dad was so focused on maintaining a steady high that he couldn't detect
my anxiety—I needed him to be OK because he was all I had. I needed
what we were doing to be OK because I needed to see him as in control.

I trusted my and Dad's connection over everything, and it saw us
through. Ours was a spiritual union of inner child and old soul, friends

for many lifetimes. Involving a child in what is, at the end of the day, a crime, is unethical. I embroider these tales with charm and magic because *that's how I experienced them.* The trickster is a threshold being between two realms—one foot planted here, the other beyond.

The letter and the spirit.

⁘

Nothing under the sun was off-limits for my exposure. It was all blinding truths, all the time, with Preston. I was always welcome to ask questions, and I did, which is how I found out my mother was a prostitute.

From the moment she crossed the California state line, Anna was off like a racehorse, chasing that rabbit wherever it ran. And it ran fast. Those drugs were *good,* and for the first time, she was around people who vibrated at her frantic pace. It must've been exhausting. The only times I remember her appearing at all in my earliest years in LA with Dad, she'd materialize upon our living room floor like magic—as though Alice herself had fallen through the rabbit hole and *THUMP!* collapsed upon the carpet in a glittery heap. I knew better than to poke that beautiful, slumbering dragon. I'd watch her sleep and snoop through her purse, looking for candy and clues about this strange beast. Only once did I mistake a handful of pills for sweets. This misstep sent me to the hospital and set me on a loop for a few days, glued to my tricycle, doing donuts like a bat outta hell on that teensy patio.

Anna hooked to make money to buy drugs, to sink deeper into that place she felt safest: the dark, in danger. I remember some parking lot meetup between Mom and Dad where I watched her, all spangled and painted up, emerge from a fancy Cadillac. I sat crisscross-applesauce upon the parked Triumph, trying to catch her eye, but she didn't look at me, not once. From the driver's side climbed a man done up like a caricature, a real true Hollywood pimp with a cane and a big hat with an ostrich feather. I was enthralled by all the glitter. Surely, she could see some shine in me, too, my little heart hoped. From that day, I begged and begged to visit her. Eventually, Preston surrendered.

I'd imagined Mom's apartment as a swanky salon-boudoir with flocked wallpaper and feathers everywhere. Instead, I walked into a dim and sparse room, speed-freak spotless, with tapestries strewn over every window, blocking the light. She shared the place with her pimp—a crash pad and control center. Cold, but for all my faith in that storm of a woman sitting on the sofa, allowing me to come near. Her foot dangling from the couch never stopped bouncing, but there she was, awake, alert, and present. For a few sweet minutes, my little three-year-old fingers clumsily knotted braids in my mother's hair, which was long for the first and last time.

It was true heaven for me, that moment, interrupted by a battering ram. In a matter of seconds, the front door splintered with a sudden crack at the hinges, and a mayhem of men in FBI flak jackets swarmed. We hit the deck as they scrambled, shouting, searching for something they found quickly: a stash of machine guns stuffed in a coat closet. They handled this arsenal and handcuffed my mom, picked me up, and carried me out to the sound of her cries and the sight of her half-braided mane. Over the officer's shoulder, I watched some heretofore-hidden housecat run from the gaping front door in terror. I sat on a curb in the parking lot, looking for that cat until the officials could figure out where I belonged.

∴

I was shaken, but a child's resilience is quick. Underwritten by the divine forgiveness that surges hope through our very veins. The memory of playing with my mother's hair held more sway in my heart than any FBI raid. I clung to it as I had those strands. When I saw Mom again, she'd chopped her locks into a curly bob, and she was on a mission.

She'd somehow skated the legal consequences of harboring smuggled weapons and popped into mine and Dad's Hollywood duplex like nothing ever happened. I was both happy to see her and mighty confused. I'd been lying on my tummy, coloring, minding my own when suddenly Anna was there, guns blazing a mile a minute. She insisted I wear some ridiculous frilly dress complete with matching ruffle-butt panties.

Oh, hell no.

My father wasn't around, or if he was, he was certainly passed out cold. I had no clue what Anna was going on about and, anyway, that dress was no good for motorcycle riding or tree climbing. Plus, no matter what I wore on the outside then, I only wore little boxer short undies underneath. And that was that.

Mom agreed to ditch the dress but kept on about those stupid fucking panties. At some point, I just stood up and stomped my foot—the same foot that had popped right outta her the night I was born; the one my father had discovered was the key to my breathing. Stamp of life, reverberating: *NO*.

Putting your foot down is the first step in taking a stand. And it set off something in my mother that was just pure vile rage. Anna went out back and got a switch, then came back in and beat me. Hard. When I still refused to wear the panties, Mom just fucking lost it—threw me to the floor and, with all her weight and wrath behind, shoved a pillow over my face. When I squirmed and kicked, she just pushed down harder.

Eventually, I surrendered. Startled, she removed the pillow. My breath came in gulps.

She'd always swatted at me, but this was something new. Mom's attacks were usually a symptom of her inner weather, things I had no control over. This time, I'd made a simple choice, sprung from what made sense to me as a child—boxers or panties—and for it, she tried to kill me.

It wouldn't be the last time. I was only three years old.

It would take years to actualize that tiny revolution, my defiant foot stepping into myself, but the journey had begun. The standoff could've been about anything, really. That it was about clothes is a minor detail that nonetheless set in motion the unfolding of my future.

∴

The Pink Pussycat was a burlesque club on Santa Monica Boulevard, a bright pink building on the outside with pink everywhere inside. The dancers had clever stage names played off of members of the Rat Pack, and all manner of rock stars and Hollywood actors strutted in and out around the clock. It was where my mother worked and it became the safest and most supervised place for me to see her.

For a while, I didn't want to see Anna at all, but once I started asking after her, the Pussycat was where Dad would take me. We'd zoom on the Triumph to that windowless pink box, and he'd drop me right at the front door. Inside was this shimmering otherworld blaring rock music. Low lit sequins sent little glimmers through the cigarette smoke, and everyone wore sunglasses and smiled big and talked loud. I'd slip past drunk young starlets at teetering bar tables, stacked with highball glasses and parapher-nalia, and head straight to the bar where the bartender knew how to make just what I liked: a Shirley Temple with extra cherries. I stabbed at the candy-red Maraschino orbs with a tiny plastic sword and ate 'em till my lips glowed crimson.

My mom wasn't nothin' to sneeze at. Striking, very tall, high cheek-bones, dark hair and eyes, olive-skinned. Beautiful hands and feet and gorgeous legs. Once I sat right next to Janis Joplin herself as we wordlessly watched my mom shimmy. I'll never forget the singer's fuzzy coat, her stacks of bracelets, and the filigree tattoo on her wrist.

When Mom finished dancing, she'd come and sit with me and order an ice-cold Tecate with lime. There was never any talk of anything of conse-quence, as though nothing had happened between us. She was just happy, the daughter of a Ferris wheel operator, exuberant and young, putting on her own show. I'll never truly know which alter was which, but the Anna who danced I liked best.

I sat at her side, listening to the goings-on at the Pussycat until, at some point, it was time for me to go. I'd dare to nuzzle my head into Mom's bare stomach for a second and wait outside 'til Dad pulled up on our chariot, and we headed home.

I had a missing Mama heart but a belly full of cherries and a sunset ride to rival any fine art.

∴

A four-year-old shouldn't have to seek sanctuary; children are meant to depend on their caregivers like the sun coming up. But the sunrise itself *was* the only thing I could count on, a lesson my dad told me explicitly many times, despite himself.

I'd begun to rely more and more upon the little mirror I held beneath Dad's nose for proof of life. I was hypnotized by the humidity that fogged and receded upon its surface, lulled into something like reassurance but just as bored as could be. I knew Preston bristled at that b-word, but what the fuck, man. I'd occupied myself with as much as I could within the confines of our space, clumsily nailing boards together and drawing and drawing and drawing. I knew that just outside our doorstep was all that bright life that had summoned my parents to California in the first place.

So, I took little pilgrimages around our neighborhood. All alone, wandering through West Hollywood, stopping here and there to pet friendly dogs or pick blooms like a proper flower child. Dad had often taken me to the Hari Krishna Temple near us, where I knew I could get a free bowl of lentils, rice, and a little cup of tea. A child hungry in all senses memorizes the landmarks that lead to comfort; I found my way to the Temple multiple times a week.

The food was wonderful, but I was fulfilled by so much more than that there. People from so many walks of life sat together on the soft lawns, dressed in crimson and saffron robes, playing these strange instruments and swaying and chanting. The scent of sandalwood mixed with Nag Champa incense, and everywhere you looked were gold-framed pictures of bright blue baby Krishna smiling or sticking out his neon-pink tongue.

No one really asked after my parents. For better or worse, in those free love days, there were lots of kids who kind of just floated around, alone or in packs, accidentally ingesting hallucinogens at times between bowls of bear mush. For the most part, our parents had just wanted to believe in something bigger than they'd been brought up to obey. In their misguided ways, they wanted better for everyone, but some didn't escape the dark side of all that light.

∴

At some point, my father woke up.

Noticing my little mirror at his bedside, he searched for me through the apartment and around the block. Upon his Triumph in the blinding sunshine, somehow, he spied me all alone, humming home from the temple. It broke his heart wide open; he scooped me up like a duckling, and we rode home. A golden opportunity to start over.

Dad was tired of paying for his addiction. The pills might've been free, but the heroin was expensive. The cost of it all was too high and too human. He tried the Twelve Steps and got to about number four when he realized he was in too deep and couldn't take care of me anymore.

We didn't have money for a rehab facility, but in those days, addicts could get clean at the state hospital, which is what he planned to do. Leaving me with Anna was unthinkable. Dad's Narcotics Anonymous sponsor, a "good, responsible man" with a family, offered to take me in for a little while, and Preston figured it was the best we could do.

Man, I was so fuckin' pissed.

How long are you gonna be gone? I cried, afraid of any answer.

I dunno, he said, *but I promise I'll be back.*

⁘

My first thought was how much I'd miss those rides through the canyons, the poetry readings, nature walks, and just him, my every single thing in the world. Now I was in this stupid perfect house full of total squares: the father was a pilot and the mother a strict homemaker, church on Sunday, baths every single day, and eat everything on your plate. Not an art supply in sight, and two kids of their own who hated everything about me and let me know it.

The food was nice, and the bed was soft. They took care of my physical needs, but my soul was withering. After a while, I started packing my suitcase each day with my little Daniel Boone coat, Dad's white Hanes V-neck T-shirt that I slept in, and my favorite moccasins. I'd put the case by the front door and sit on it, twirling my ragged-red umbrella as I sat in the sun, waiting and waiting. And every damn day, the lady of the house would unpack it, getting snappier each time.

I remember thinking that if Dad didn't come back for me, then I'd rather be dead.

This just couldn't be my life.

Fear of abandonment still shoves its sudden spike in my heart sometimes, cold. Back then, it manifested as hope, which sometimes masquerades as stubbornness. The last time I packed my little suitcase, that lady told me to go out back and get a switch because she was gonna whip me. I dawdled in the yard, taking my time finding just the dinkiest twig. When I got back to the front porch, she'd gone inside, so I sat back down on the suitcase, tracing knots in the wooden porch floor with the little stick. Its light scratches, sight and sound, stirred a soothing in my ear and chest until the air all around vibrated like the deep hum of a motorcycle engine.

It had been six months, but my father had returned.

.•.

One definition of the word triumph is "great victory," which implies that a battle has been fought and won. Dad was clean. He strapped my little suitcase onto the back of our motorcycle, and I climbed up on the gas tank, glaring at the well-meaning family waving goodbye. I may as well have flipped them the bird. I felt like a damn champion, all redemption and rainbow-sparkle *see-ya*! There was so much behind me and Dad, so much between us, and always the road ahead. We were each other's heroes, and we could conquer anything.

I settled into a muscle-memory position as Preston climbed on behind me. I didn't know where we were going and didn't care, until he shouted in my ear over the engine revving, *Kid, we're headed off. Your mom's pregnant, and she's gonna have the baby.* This red-flag news was fourth-of-July fireworks for me. How Dad sensed the child in Anna's womb shared his blood, I have no clue, but into Anna's little duplex, on La Cienega Drive in LA, we headed. Holy holy, I couldn't be happier or more hopeful. We chased down the sunset back to my mother, drawn to the new life within. For all my eyes couldn't see, my heart could perceive. The organ that forms first, that speaks loudest. Bulging straight from our chests, bright as maraschino cherries and brave as anything.

∴

When we say something's faded, it's usually in regards to memory or light. A lessening of brightness or vitality, a weakening. Light erodes material—photos, fabric—but doesn't lessen them; it lends them a new facet. So many sunrises and sunsets have to happen to achieve a specific hue or perspective that didn't exist before. One that we can hold in our hands or wear upon our breast as evidence of our weathering, talismans of our survival.

Bolts of fabric, twisted into circles beneath the searing sun. Wearing something our star has touched and transformed might not seem like much in the face of trauma, but it reorients me to warmth, to the recollections of when and where I felt most connected to the planet, to my father, to myself.

It's the mercy in our making that allows for these kinds of memories to win over the dark ones. Though they might haunt us and protect us from harm, bad memories will always be lessened by those of light. Our survival depends on these rays of built-in grace, the thriving that urges us to hope.

Chapter 3

STITCHED SONGBIRDS

"The Serenity Prayer"
God,
grant me the serenity
to accept the things I cannot change,
the courage to change the things I can,
and the wisdom to know the difference.
Amen.

—REINHOLD NEIBHUR

SOMETIMES, AN ESCAPE IS ALSO A RETURN.

In the animal world, after a creature undergoes something traumatic, they go off somewhere and tremble. They "shake it off," discharging the energy and completing the nervous system response. Everything gets reset, and they return to the present moment.

When Preston and I came back to Anna on the Triumph, everything was shaky. Both my parents were clean for the first time in my lifetime, and it was like: now that things were clear, things became clear, ya know? Sober, Dad realized, *wow*. For all Anna's twisted shit, at least when they were doing drugs, they had a lot of fun together: you're high, that person's

· 29 ·

high, it's all a big masquerade. Now that they were sober, sticking to the steps and calling their sponsors and one day at a time, that mask slowly dissolved.

Mom's agile alters defied sobriety entirely. These weren't simply masks: the personalities were ingrained survival mechanisms. We had no name for these ceaseless switches, no perspective in which to view them objectively. We were just subject to their various charms and abuses, and the only way Dad and I could figure to stay was by, every so often, escaping.

Back on the Triumph, the bike's growing velocity balanced with the slow, stable transformation of nature. It got us back to good and brought us both the serenity to accept the things we could not change. That first phrase of the Serenity Prayer is the path Preston and I walked with bare feet, toe-hold clinging with each step to the shifting sand.

There's not really any bad news in nature. What we call catastrophe, to nature, is just neutral. Preston always said if you can't find the space to get to love, even toward yourself, at least be neutral. Everything else'll just make you sick and turn you into that thing you don't understand or don't wanna be.

All I wanted to be, then, was by Dad's side on that bright shore of belief, awaiting my soon-to-be brother. And, despite it all, with my mother, turbulent and turning—nature herself, in one fluctuating form.

∴

On the eve of my fifth birthday in September 1968, I stayed behind with Anna as Preston zipped off on the bike. Some small offense had vexed him, and he'd snuck away to tremble. It was strange that I didn't join him, but Anna buzzed around, fixing to bake me a cake and planning a big party for the next day. I was always wary of Mom's kindness, but I hoped. Because for a second, our life on La Cienega Boulevard was pretty peachy, considering.

Two actors occupied the other side of the duplex we lived in—talented, artful, gay men who held the lead roles in LA's production of the musical *Hair*. They were geniuses, generous with their time and energy, and, more importantly, their endless stash of wigs, scarves, and fringe. Plus, they had two dogs I adored: giant fuzzy standard poodles, one puffy white and another inky black. I spent a lot of time over there, rolling around on the old wooden floors, all decked out like a little hippie, giggling with those giant, playful pups. It felt warm and safe and creative and encouraging— the polar opposite of the house full of squares I'd recently escaped from. It reset my whole system; even Mom couldn't help but relax into it every so often.

That evening, Mom had gone over to the neighbors' to grab a cake pan. I sat on my butt in front of our tiny TV, sucked into some late-1960s horror show that, as the sun faded, threw shadows and echoed shrieks through our bare-ass apartment. The darker it got, the more the fear burned up in my throat. I was a hardy kid, but I was barely almost five, and at some point, it was just too much for me. Some jump-scare electrified me and I ran straight next door, bursting into the scene as a bundle of freaked-out kid energy.

I remember like a crack that sharp wooden slap of the screen door behind me, then immediately a snarling tangle of teeth and black-and-white fur ripping up my face and scalp. By the time the neighbors managed to pull the dogs off me, I was a big bloody mess. There were shouts and panic and my own blood everywhere. I was rushed into the back of another neighbor's car with a towel wrapped around my face; stunned and muffled, I was in total shock.

Some charitable hospital took me in and put three hundred stitches in my face and head. Bandages wrapped my swollen skull. Everything hurt. We were too poor to stay long at the hospital, so the doctors just sutured me up and sent me home with antibiotics.

I felt sore and sorry and sad for startling the dogs. I didn't know where my dad was, and all my mother could do was repeat how it was all my fault. I'd ruined my own birthday, but she still wanted that damn party. I grabbed my little nightlight and laid down on the floor of my closet, pulled the door shut, and stayed there for months.

∴

Some entity within Anna delighted in the idea of throwing a big celebration as her daughter sat locked in a closet. It was the manifestation of
some looking-glass wish she'd made as a child herself, locked away in the
dark—a twisted rewrite that set something right with one of her alters.

I heard people coming and going through the closet door, music and
laughter and carrying on. No one came to check on me, but that was okay.
All I wanted was my dad. Finally, above it all, I heard the puttering of his
Triumph; the sound pulled me up from where I lay, and for the first time,
I dared to touch the threads that held my face together. I was afraid of
how my dad might react when he saw me. I had no idea what I looked like.

A few minutes later, Preston knocked lightly and entered at my mumble.
He sat right down, put his arm around me, and presented me with a small
piece of my birthday cake. Its number five candle glowed brightly in the
darkness, dancing to the tune of his singing "Happy Birthday." He told
me to make a wish, and at that moment, I couldn't think of a single thing
better than him by my side.

We sat like that for I don't know how long, eating our cake. I chewed in
tiny bites, the small sweetness and the scent of my dad, my true celebration.
I didn't wanna come out, didn't wanna see anyone. The only thing that got
me to show my face was the voices of my neighbors, who had shown up so
very sorry. I heard them asking Anna about me and saying they planned to
put the dogs down. Every cell in my soul screamed *NO! NO!*

You could never do that! I shouted as I rushed into the kitchen. *It wasn't
their fault!*

My voice was garbled and strange and far-away sounding to my ears,
wrapped in gauze. Everyone at the party froze. I felt all their eyes upon me,
this crazy-looking, stitched-up kid with blood-stained blonde curls. The
sight of me probably really fucked up some of the heavier trippers in that
room that day, but I stamped my little foot and stood fast. Our neighbors
fled, and Anna narrowed her eyes on me and Preston, who stood with his
hand on my shoulder. The party was over.

I returned to the closet, where I listened to guests leaving, then the
clanging of cake pans and glasses in the sink, and the shattering of Anna

and Preston fighting. Later, once the sun had gone down and all was silent, I opened the door a peep. Preston was gone and Anna was passed out.

I grabbed a blanket and tiptoed my way through the kitchen, careful not to awaken the spiteful sleeping dragon whose party I'd ruined. My face was hot and my heart was tired; I wanted to lay in the cool night, beneath the California stars.

Softly, so as not to upset any living thing, I whispered to the dogs I prayed were out there. One glowing ball of fluff and her opaque shadow shyly approached the fence, head down and tail wagging. I poked my five-year-old hand through one of those woven wire diamonds and let the dogs sniff and lick me as I just cried and cried. My face ached so bad but I couldn't stop telling them both how sorry I was for scaring them and putting them in a bad spot.

Those dogs had been frightened, plain and simple, just like I was. They'd sensed my fear and reacted from theirs. Now, they sensed my forgiveness. Their wet noses in my palm were the sincerest of apologies, and we three sat there in our shushed and soppy healing for I don't know how long.

∴

Mom never liked what she saw when she looked at me, and after the attack, it only got worse. I'd emerge from the closet to eat or use the bathroom, but Anna rarely, if ever, popped her head in to check on me. Somehow, I'd held up another mirror to her childhood; with each passing year, some new startling facet appeared through my sheer existence.

Now, I was a legit monster, and it wasn't just Anna who said so.

I'd always been this outsider kid with crazy artist-junkie parents. My teeth were crooked and janky, and my hair was insane. I wore whatever I wanted most of the time and barely bathed. I'd never really cared what other people thought of me. But once the bandages were removed, any little outing made the shock of my appearance undeniable. Scars tore across my face in violent plum slashes, pinching my expressions, accentuating my other wacky characteristics. Adults would flinch before catching themselves and expressing concern. Kids were just outright jerks: *What HAPPENED to your FACE? Are you a MONSTER?*

I felt like a freak, and then I felt bad about feeling like a freak. When Dad visited me in my isolation, he'd try to soothe me with treats and books and the fact that, *Hey, some people don't even have eyes, kid.*

Nevertheless, these things shape our self concept. I took to turning off the light when I went into the bathroom and avoided mirrors. I still do, overall. I'm drawn to mirrors that are crazed, hazy, cracked, or straight-up shattered and rearranged into a disco ball—those that reflect a kind of distortion. Because if those months I spent in the closet when I was five taught me anything, it's that we certainly can't control how others see us and we often can't even see ourselves correctly. We get hung up on what we perceive as "flaws," ignoring our true and radiant nature.

The only creatures that didn't bat an eye at me for some time were animals, my father, and, finally, my brand-new baby brother.

∴

My brother Thovas was born on June 25, 1969, about a month before man landed on the moon.

He was a sickly little baby, tiny and needy and sweet. I'd been sickly and small, too, but for some reason, in all the places Mom was offended by me, she was just delighted by Thovas. He, in turn, adored Anna. Their bond was something that, instead of jealousy, washed over me with relief—at least for a little bit, I was off the hook.

My brother's thin little fingers followed my scars like lines on a map— the topography of the chaos he'd been born into but also the healing that couldn't be hidden. It was hard for other people to see so blatantly, but Thovas couldn't give a care what my face looked like; he just wanted to be held, be sung to. His presence in the world brought me out of my own gestation, reborn and reemergent, ready for our family's new adventure.

We were leaving Los Angeles. There were just too many ghosts and temptations lurking around those hills and old haunts; it wasn't an easy place for Anna and Preston to stay straight, to say the least. My dad's hands were getting itchy, and instead of safes or hair or heroin, he yearned to get 'em dirty, immerse them in the soil—to stay and kneel and pay attention and watch something grow. So when I was about six-years-old, we all moved to Northern California, to a little town called Sebastopol.

∴

Preston sold the Triumph and replaced our fair chariot with a big rig, old and rusty and cool. He hand-painted Bugs Bunny caricatures on the truck's massive, creaky doors. It was a new ride for lugging organic fertilizer and landscaping supplies. I'd climb into the cab, and Dad and I'd drive out to Mendocino or the Russian River, where we'd camp and swim, and Preston would lug his telescope for us to watch the stars and planets on clear nights.

But our favorite retreat was the Redwood Forest; it became mine and Dad's second home, the trees themselves like part of the family—those massive master spirits with the funny fiddlehead ferns at their feet that resembled our own crazy hair. It felt like Preston and I had the place to ourselves; sometimes, we wouldn't see another human soul. We'd run around the enormous trunks looking for fairies and talking to God. It was just more than I could ever take in, the beauty of it all.

But really, we were completely immersed in nature in Sebastopol. We didn't need to escape to it—it was just everywhere. Right outside the house we rented, this cute old 1910s shiplap California country cottage, the land rolled and rose and reminded you. Our time in Sebastopol was my parents' first wholehearted stab at clean living and the only real happy time our family ever had. It was the first time I'd witnessed either of my parents be *aware of* and *susceptible to* the weather. Seeing Mom and Dad in their star-appliquéd, embroidered denim jackets seared into my memory every picture of health. We ate somewhat normal food at a more-or-less predictable time most days. There was some structure, a tiny sliver of reliability, and just fistfuls of beauty.

Twelve-step meetings were Anna and Preston's only adult social outings, then. That part of California attracts lots of motorcyclists, the kind of folk Dad was especially drawn to. Hard-living big dudes with patches on their leather vests to prove it, over the hangover routine, with the Big Book and a worn copy of *Zen and the Art of Motorcycle Maintenance* stuffed in their saddlebags. The one Thanksgiving we had in Sebastopol—the first and last proper, cheerful one for many years—I came home from a bicycle ride to find motorcycles all over our yard. There were about twenty Hell's Angels in our house (you can't just invite one Hell's Angel), helping Anna cook and passing Thovas around like a sack of potatoes.

Before, when it was just Dad and me, holidays had been spent down on Skid Row. I'd ask Preston why we were doing this, and he answered we were going to help the less fortunate. My reply became our running joke—*But Dad, how could anyone be less fortunate than us?*

But I knew what he meant, and it stuck. That year in Sebastopol, we took in strays—people who didn't have family, people in recovery. Even Anna was on board with the hubbub of a full house. Those times are trapped in amber: making crafts and ornaments from paper and glitter, gifts of treasures found in nature, and family from strangers.

⁘

Then we moved again.

It wasn't a geographical cure or even a bummer, really. Mom and Dad had the opportunity to be caretakers of a ranch in an even smaller North California town called Forestville. We'd live in a three-story 1800s Victorian house on acres and acres of gorgeous land. It was a yellow heaven of sun-drenched daffodils, with a big friendly cow I could ride and hundreds of peacocks making kaleidoscopes of the trees.

The house was old and creaky and didn't have electricity or a proper bathroom. We used chamber pots like Oliver Twist, bathed outside, and washed our clothes in the water hose or the creek like Huck Finn. Our duties were to shepherd the livestock, keep the house lived-in, and fix whatever needed fixing.

It was all I ever wanted. I built a rickety but real treehouse with old boards and went to what was called a "free school," where I didn't even have to wear shoes. My brother toddled behind me at all times, and we hardly ever went inside. 'Cuz from the moment Thovas walked, my mother all but disappeared.

Mom never shined to nature, not any of it, not ever. Sometimes the sky is just too big, the sun too bright for certain people. Anna couldn't alchemize all that light; from childhood, she was attuned to darkness. Help for those experiencing mental illness in the early 1970s fell extremely short and failed many. The local doctor Mom saw shrugged off her symptoms as the effects of anxiety—housewife hysteria. Scripts of Valium and sleeping pills knocked her out, mummifying her within the pain. She'd get up a little to look after Thovas, but otherwise, she stayed in bed with the shades drawn.

In those days, people didn't say the word *trauma*. Veterans were just *shell-shocked*. Abused women were *asking for it*. Abused kids were a dime a dozen. You went on with what you were given and got thrown into an institution when you couldn't cope. Mental illness was a blurry concept and a real bad word.

All Mom's usual distractions were gone in Forestville: no drugs, no dancing, nothing doing. No meetings or Hell's Angels or spontaneous, inappropriate birthday parties. There was no putting it off anymore. The wildfire was coming and we all knew it, but we were lulled into magical thinking by the surrounding beauty: the hope that maybe tragedy would sidestep us this time. This one time. Please.

∴

When you're burning inside, anything is tinder—open hills, daffodils. The glint of peacock feathers startles instead of soothes; the sheer volume of brightness oppresses. Your own children's laughter, their very breath, mocks the mayhem in your brain, howling for it all to be painted black.

I was always attracted to little scurrying things. I stashed homemade Mason jar terrariums with bugs and spiders and lizards all over my room, even though Anna forbade it. She couldn't stand the thought of sharing space with all those confined, creeping creatures.

One day, I came across a garter snake that I just had to keep. I didn't know how else to get it up to my room, so I smuggled the snake inside my mouth, slithering and writhing, bold and fearful as my own tongue. But Mom's senses were razor sharp; she didn't miss a thing. When I tried to shuffle past her, she demanded I answer some random question. She never engaged me with anything, never asked me shit. The second I parted my lips, the snake popped right out, sparking a switchblade reflex in Mom that set to slapping me.

I don't know how long she went for, just beating and beating me. My mother could get that way like she was somewhere else. Sometimes, the beatings would last for a good hour until she stopped cold. She wanted something from me that I refused to give her: a response, a plea.

Instead, I just went somewhere else, too. Covered my head and curled into my belly, silent as the little snake I watched ric-rac slither out the wide-open screen door into the sunshine.

∴

Anna was more adept at finding beauty everywhere than anyone I've ever met but, for her, the nature we were surrounded by in Northern California didn't offer the materials she craved. It was all too gentle, too clean, and too quiet.

To create her art, Anna needed grit.

Like an oyster, Mom took the gnarl she found into her darkness and trembled around it, washing and skinning and shining and alchemizing it until it became a pearl. This was her only health. Devoid of that process, surrounded only by softness, she clamped shut and stayed that way. She was a city bird who only knew how to make nests out of plastic six-pack rings, stray ribbons, cigarette butts, and shredded paper.

About a month after Mom beat me for the snake, Dad said it'd be best if we all moved back to Texas. Anna wasn't gonna get better out in California. I was pretty pissed, but I wanted more than anything for my mom to be well. And, beneath and despite it all, Anna wanted her mother. It was this circular, swirling wish that Louise would finally somehow step up and say she was sorry and do right by her daughter.

Fuck, how I understood that. More than how I understood our return to Texas would make me the new kid in school with a crazy face, the weirdo who belonged barefoot in a treehouse and doing her business in a chamber pot.

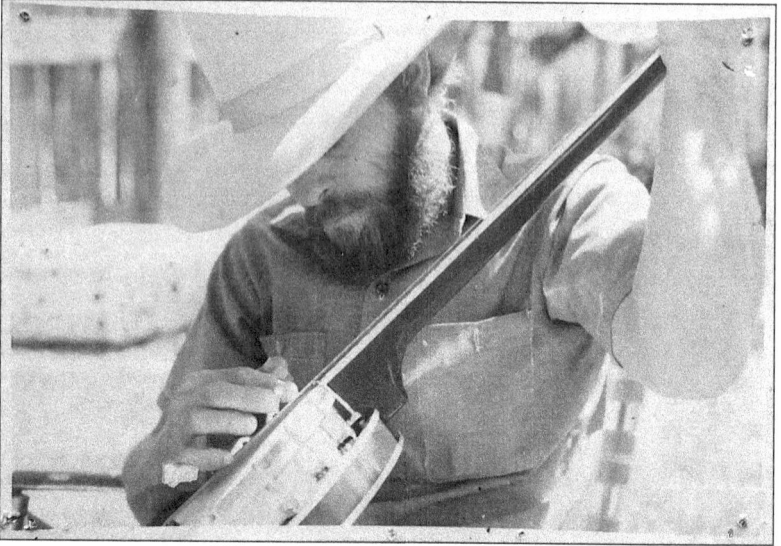

Preston and his banjo.

∴

Since the Triumph and the Bugs Bunny truck, our means of transportation shifted into a string of beat-up vehicles that held less and less sentimentality, no matter their personality. At that time, we had a knock-around station wagon with wooden panels packed with our sparse belongings. We weren't allowed to bring anything besides clothes and maybe one stuffed animal. Thovas had left behind his beloved fire truck, a strawberry-red metal contraption he could scoot around on, with a brass bell that went *ding! ding! ding!* He was heart-fuckin'-broken about that thing and cried about it most of the way.

I'd ushered all my hidden pets from their enclosures and set them scuttling free but kept one Mason jar to fill with the rocks and sea glass Dad and I'd collected on our escapes. It wasn't permitted, but I wrapped it in a shirt and shoved it under the seat. Somewhere along the way, the jar jostled free, and Preston heard my contraband telltale clatter. He pulled right over and dumped each one on the roadside, smashed the jar, and off we went.

Thovas's tears traded for mine, silent and stinging, flowing down the river beds of scars on my face. I looked out the window and watched it all just keep moving, keep changing, and keep happening, all beautiful and neutral. Preston's favorite adage: *If you focus on what you don't have and what you can't keep, you're just turning your back on everything being offered to you by the handful.* The rocks weren't mine; I was theirs.

At that point in my life, I'd learned there wasn't much use feeling sorry for myself, even as my heart felt like that Mason jar on the side of the road, slivers of shattered glass. We're all shuttling stones beneath our seats, silently hoping no one will hear 'em rolling around. Not a single one of us is free from pain. Dad saw it and said it plain; I took it on the chin, which I rested on top of my little brother's head as we snuggled up in the back seat. The promise of my brother had pulled me from the darkness of my closet after the dog attack. The whisper of my witness, who'd accept me just as I was and still does.

I held Thovas's little hand and hummed his bedtime song as the night grew dark, and he drifted to sleep in my arms. It was a scrap of bright hope named for a scarce, short-lived flower, a tune from *The Sound of Music*, which Thovas and I had reenacted on repeat, twirling atop and rolling down those Northern California hills.

Edelweiss, may you bloom and grow, bloom and grow forever.

∴

If an animal doesn't alchemize their trauma, they shut down. Instinct injured, no way to return to their nature, which is just to keep going. Their continuance transmits and emboldens us humans to do the same.

I hoped returning to San Antonio would reinvigorate Mom and Dad; neither had really made any art for some time, for the first time in my life. I hoped their hands would find the right materials to shake it all out and start fresh.

The courage to change the things we can.

*We don't have the automatic tremble response as our animal friends do. We have to **want to** keep going and find ways to make it possible. Nature and* *her animals bear witness to us, and we bear witness to each other, and this is how we transmit the trauma out of us. Incremental processes, shrinking our tonal to what we can create, stitch by stitch, to show God we're still here, we're paying attention, and we can't do it without their higher power and each other. A plea and a push, our participation. It's all necessary.*

I sew this into everything I make, a motif in my life and my work in a language of appliquéd roses and hand-stitched rabbits, birds sewn and drawn in flight as they were in life. It rarely feels much like courage at all, or at least not in the way people define the word. It's tiny, and sometimes it feels like it's not enough, but I promise you it's the only thing. It's everything.

If the birds keep on making nests, if they know there's gonna be a tomorrow, then I wanna stick around and see what they're singing about. They're who I'm gonna listen to—over the bad news and the berating voice in my head that clicks on like a Groundhog Day alarm first thing every morning.

The wisdom to know the difference.

Soaring and free, forever at home, singing some promise only our hearts can interpret. I had no idea what my family would face in San Antonio, but I figured, at the very least, there'd be birds.

We arrive in this life, as creators,.
As children we know how to make
how to carve; how to take one thing
and alchemize it into something different
Stars and colors and light spread
through our beings and into our waking worlds
Our work as adults is to never forget this.
We must never forget this.

Chapter 4

SILVER MOON BOOTS

SAN ANTONIO REANIMATED MOM. INSTANTLY, SHE STARTED wearing makeup again, platform boots, and all kinds of wigs. Stacks of jangly jewelry that announced her, echoed her, put sound to her frantic vibration. She was revived, even relieved. Mom's appearance was part of her art—alchemy with an intention somewhere between RuPaul and Ram Dass.

The moment her platforms hit the pavement, she and Preston opened a store. I wasn't allowed to bring a fucking jar of rocks, but my parents tried to import the feel of the whole state of California back to San Antonio by opening a store they named Banana Funk N' Junk. I have no idea how they got the scratch to start a business; no idea how Mom rallied through the bottles of Valium that just kept growing taller and emptying faster.

But Anna put every single shred of energy she had into that place. Maybe it was mild mania, a little storm in sequins. The line winds when it comes to creativity and mental illness. But a flatline is always exactly what it is. Sometimes, you have to embrace a little madness in art, and my mom was fully committed.

Nothing was static, all electric. Even though Dad missed the wide-open California sunshine, Anna's excitement jump-started his system. Mom and

Dad were only ever really happy together if they were creating; it was the only time they functioned as partners. Banana was a hive for their spirits, a psych-rock atmosphere that hummed like a sewing machine, records playing on repeat, a stream of visitors. Like they had years ago at the beauty salon, Anna and Preston crafted a vibe that drew people in, and the buzz drowned out the darkness for a bit.

∴

The shop was in an old two-story building right smack in the middle of San Antonio, on the corner of Flores and Ashby, near San Pedro Park. Our family moved into the walk-up apartment right above Banana. The feel of the store rose through the floorboards; murals from below continued their patterns above, tying everything together.

Life then was a revolving art show—everything was fair game for embellishment. Embroidered flames crept up the sides of bell-bottom jeans, and old tapestries took on the form of sculptural, life-size Virgin Mary dolls. Dad made detailed paintings of Indigenous American and Chicano heroes; Mom did abstracts. They painted walls, canvases, clothing, and furniture.

What my parents didn't transform, they sold "as is"—those two little words that carry so many scars and such heart.

The phrase itself felt like me, like our life. It felt like enough.

Little porcelain cups—just slightly chipped, hand-tatted lace gloves with century-old stains—the marks of the movement of time, arcs of story that landed in our little shop, up for grabs. These objects moved us to tears and transferred through our fingers as currency. They were so vulnerable out there on display. But someone was always seeking that one outcast thing, stumbling upon it in a moment of recognition, choosing it, and bringing it into their life.

I learned from this flow of objects the concept of true belonging, which isn't a place, but a practice. Those little things didn't belong to us or even to the people who purchased them. They were both a part of a whole and stood on their own in all their glorious brokenness, perfect exactly as they were. There was a sacredness in that, an authenticity that resonated with me, helped me to recognize me, and still does.

∴

I was a total outsider when I started third grade in San Antonio public schools. The other kids made it pretty plain. I struggled to make friends, to pay attention, to sit still. I wanted to belong, but I just didn't. It wasn't just my teeth and face and hair anymore. Now, it was the way I dressed that brought so much violence, and that was something that came home with me.

Though home had become this sort of thriving, pulsing studio where art was nurtured and held most high, my parents never ever encouraged my expression through fashion. They both despised everything I put on my body for completely different reasons. My clothes triggered this visceral response from them both, centered on my gender and how nearly what I wore might have mirrored my mother's style.

If I wore tomboy stuff, Anna would get angry. She wanted me to look like a pretty girl, a flashy doll she could fashion, or else I should just disappear. For Dad, anything interesting I wore was causing too much of a stir, bringing too much attention. It was his responsibility to make sure I didn't become like my mother, and that started with what I put on my body.

No matter what my parents did or said to challenge that one aspect of my individuality, I stood firm. I was gonna get beat by Anna or made fun of at school or told to change by Dad, anyway. I had learned it by watching my parents, after all: the only way to survive what was roiling within you and stacked outside against you was by staying true to the creative inspiration that visits you. I absorbed and incorporated and transformed both of my parents' aesthetics, as well as the methods and materials of my grandparents, but through what I wore, I belonged entirely to myself.

And I wanted Silver Moon Boots.

∴

I've always been possessed by shoes. They protect and proclaim our path, our stance. They dance and dig in and form to our feet like second-skin stompers that become our companions. My feet had saved my life in so many ways at that point, so it made sense. Shoes spoke to me, more than anything else, the soul of the person who wore them and the vision of the person who made them.

Dad was perennially in work boots: beat-down lace-up Timberland-type clunkers superimposed with paint splatters and mud. He'd wear them all the way through to the sole. Man, those shoes had gravity and pulled me to follow wherever they led, even if I didn't like it.

Preston was pretty pissed that I wanted those Moon Boots. Real hot shit at that time, Moon Boots were snow boots inspired by humanity's first foray into space, all puffy and tall and attention-getting—these shoes were out of our realm for a thousand reasons. Still, Dad was primarily upset that I'd desire anything so extravagant and so beyond the basics. If Thovas and I whined about wanting anything material, we'd get an earful from him. Somehow we weren't showing enough gratitude for LIFE, weren't appreciating our own sight or hands or our own feet. One summer afternoon, my brother and I had the nerve to ask Preston for a second popsicle. In response, he stopped cold at what he was doing at the shop and told us to get in the car. We had no fuckin' clue where he was headed, but we knew it wasn't good.

When we pulled into the parking lot of the Methodist hospital, we knew shit was serious. We followed Preston to the front desk, where he asked the receptionist if he could take his children down to the morgue to see a dead child. My body went cold and my eyes went wide. I knew this lady was gonna throw our crazy asses out or send Dad to the psych ward. But, lo-and-behold, she simply called down to the mortician and told us we were welcome. Through a maze of bright hallways to the deepest, coldest, most antiseptic corner of the hospital we went, pulling on Preston's T-shirt the whole time, begging. *Dad, please no, please, please, please no.*

The mortician let us in as if it were the most normal thing in the world: just a Dad teaching his kids a lesson! I heard Preston tell him, *I want my kids to put their hand on a cold dead child so they'll realize the importance of their warm life.*

We didn't have to do it, thank God—Thovas and I were in such a ter-rified and desperate state by that point, and Preston saw his message had gotten across. The freezing finality of that room made me wanna run back into the sunlight as fast as I could. The moment its warmth hit my face, I decided I'd just paint silver glitter on my own damn shoes.

⁘

Dad knew his methods were extreme, but he wanted to show us that by virtue of being healthy and alive, we could create anything our whiny, whimsical minds could come up with. He wanted us to learn empathy, that feeling into the form of another, walking in their shoes. Where creativity and empathy meet is the zone my father struggled to remain in. Banana Funk N' Junk was his bona fide ode to this.

We were a white family living in the middle of a primarily black and brown neighborhood, as we had been pretty much everywhere we had lived except Northern California. Public art was part of how people in that neighborhood took care of each other. Murals of ancestors, activists, and artists bloomed on brick walls and whitewashed fences. Altars to the Virgin Mary cropped up on street corners and inside little metal fence-lined parcels of front yards. Mom and Dad gave materials and time to these episodes of devotion, weaving our family into the community with brushstrokes, mirror shards, and embroidered anatomical hearts. Thovas and I tagged along sometimes to help or hang out. We listened to the sto-ries and picked up a little Spanish, absorbing and integrating the warmth and connection in the community.

I learned more in the Banana Funk N' Junk days than I could ever have realized. A first-rate education, on the spot and *a la mosca*, hand-to-mouth, heart-to-heart. Explicit and implicit. Day-to-day operations at the shop covered the practical stuff: counting change, handwriting, and tallying receipts. Hearing Mom and Dad barter and interact with customers was real-life social studies. The territories surrounding the shop covered the subject of geography—which abandoned buildings and houses Thovas and I could sneak into, scouting for junk or just for the hell of it. Science class was starting fires on the flat rooftops of old factories when it was cold. Our recess was breaking into the Pearl Brewery to dare hot stale sips of old pull-top cans of beer, running to the horse stables in Breckenridge Park to pet the horses, nosing our way into the cafeteria at Trinity University to steal little boxes of cereal and play the jukebox.

Once Thovas was potty-trained, he was all mine—the Oliver to my Artful Dodger, my protégé and pal, my ward, and my wonder. I taught him to forage for food, pointing out fruit trees and edible wild greens. In lean times, we figured the mechanics of breaking into vending machines with our skinny arms or bending a coat hanger to scoop loose change out from under washing machines at the laundromat. Both of us could eye which empty bottles or cans we could cash in and where they could be found. With the loot scoured from all this scavenging, we'd skip to the day-old bread store to buy Mexican pastries. My brother balanced on the handlebars of whatever rickety bike I had at the moment, we'd ride to San Pedro Park and eat every morsel of those bright, dry cookies, rolling around til' the sun set.

Often, the children of other antique dealers would join us—scrappy, wolf-eyed kids who became instant soulmates, my saviors over the years. Our little gang knew the best dumpsters in the neighborhood, and we weren't afraid to jump right in. We were part of every facet of that neighborhood. Each of us belonged. My brother and I had the cunning luck and curious spirit of our dad, the shameless need and sharp eye of our mother, and somehow, mercifully, the protection of the Divine. We never got caught or picked on or harmed out there. We always knew the real threat was brewing at home.

∴

Me, Thovas & our friend, Pandora

Thovas

Mom wasn't one to be inconvenienced by a child. Contrary to what might be considered even the most basic maternal instincts, she didn't want better for us and said so. We rarely had toothbrushes because Mom had bad teeth, so we should, too—this reasoning applied all the way down the line from hygiene to nutrition to affection. The daily maintenance of tying shoes and kissing boo-boos wasn't her thing. Once a kid could say anything more than *Mama,* she had no use for them.

Still, although my brother and I were raised exactly the same, it was somehow completely different. At the time, it was just this big invisible thing we didn't know how to talk about, the inverse relationship with our parents. Mom might not have always been loving or appropriate or even *there* for my brother, but she let him be and never raised a hand to him. He was closer to Anna, and I was closer to Preston.

I hate the word "unconditional," but if there's anything a child needs, it's knowing that someone loves them at all costs. That there's nothing they could do to make the parent's love go away. My dad would tell me, *I may not like your behavior, but I will always love you.* It was the kind of love that coursed beneath whatever rocks he could dump out. We knew it was there, but we couldn't always see it. If a kid knows they're loved to the core, it's kinda like a safety net. Our safety nets had big holes in 'em—gaps in the ropes where tensions shifted, warped, and cinched, moving and reweaving without warning.

My brother never took a shine to heights, but everywhere we went I climbed trees high as my bare feet could take me. Thovas kept his on solid ground, squinting up at me with one hand over his eyes. I learned every climbable tree in the neighborhood by toehold. At the tip-top, I'd close my eyes and imagine I was a trapeze artist in the circus, wearing this beautiful sequin outfit, soaring, sparkling, and free. Thovas's nervous little voice below always brought me back to Earth.

For all the places we needed safety, Thovas and I wove our own nets. Tied from Mark Twain and myth, the truth transformed into a series of epic, daring adventures. Our quests carved a little space in our shared existence for magic and imagination and laughter.

We clung to it like a tiny sun on days when darkness won.

❖

Salvaging clothing and furniture was a way for my family to transmute our own pain. To make something beautiful out of it, from within it. Recycling misery into magic. Every day, we rearranged the shop as things sold, and I can still hear the long metal slice of Mom's shears as she cut the sleeves off one dress to sew onto another, take the bottom of a nightgown to put onto a shirt, and so on.

It was a flux that nurtured so much, but that kind of buzz requires balance to maintain. The inverse of Anna's sequined mania was an opaque depression. Things piled up, unfinished and neglected, and at a certain point, Preston couldn't take the clutter. So we just closed up shop and moved, sold some stuff, and left the rest for the neighbors to rummage through.

My father's all-time favorite works of art were those mandalas monks make from colored sand, the ones that take months or even years to complete. Each minuscule grain of sand is attended to with so much mindfulness and precision, a meditation the monks keep with the intention of healing the community.

Working from the center outward, the monks create sacred medicine for all, not just for themselves. Regardless of the amount of time and effort spent, of the scale and breathtaking perfection, each sand painting is destroyed in the end. From the outside in, the mandalas are swept into a heap and collected in a jar, which is then wrapped in silk and carried to a river and released back into nature.

That's what closing up Banana felt like. Its imprinted alchemy still echoes through my soul.

❖

The Pearl in Magnolia Pearl comes from that time. Somewhere along the way, buckets of those baubles, real and fake and found and cultured, came into the shop. They were remnants of the sea to me, of California, of mermaid daydreams. I piled them on, their toothy, slippery click-clack following me wherever I went.

As much as both Preston and Anna despised them, the nickname stuck. They were little bits of fire around my neck and stacked up my arms, actualizing my spirit. With all that had happened and all that was to come in our family, I knew that in order to survive, I had to hold tight to who I was, the treetop trapeze me.

It wasn't in the sequins or the pearls or any actual thing, though those materials and more are direct channels for my inner child—how I communicate with her, listen to her, honor her, still. Little bits of whimsy that speak to the children in others and invite them to play, to climb, to fly. Not just for fun, but for survival, for thriving.

My father's taking me to touch a "cold, dead child" taught me something different than he'd intended. I didn't realize it in words then, but I understood that my inner child was as good as that poor kid if I let Preston, Anna, or anyone take responsibility for my life and how I expressed myself.

I never got those Moon Boots, but I did make my own. And every time I did, someone wanted 'em. I gave each pair away in a succession of silver that became my platform.

Chapter 5

PAINT AND STAINS

MY FATHER STUCK TO A PRETTY STRICT UNIFORM: WHITE Hanes V-neck tees and faded Levi's 501 jeans. It was his dependable backdrop, a blank slate that absorbed paint splatters, coffee stains, cigarette smoke, and motor oil. The choice was more than about being cool or practical. For Dad, it was spiritual, his wardrobe a worn relic—his own lyric "Man in Black" by Johnny Cash.

When Preston went to the thrift store, he'd select those old 501s with an eye to the hems. He sought pairs slightly longer than he was tall, so the cuffs caught beneath his feet with each step. The hems got dingy and frayed pretty quickly, with gray-black scuffs forever at his heels like rain clouds. Each movement forward was a little tug back to Earth, a physical reminder to not just float away but to stay and pay attention.

He'd learned the Levi trick from the Levites themselves, Old Testament holy men who wore divinely dictated garments. Each piece of the priest's ensemble spoke to some specific realm of the spirit. Preston was most drawn to the idea of the Levites' sashes—long bolts of cloth that the Levites wrapped around their waists and that dragged on the ground, constantly tripping them up as a reminder to stay rooted in human existence. To keep in mind the suffering of their fellow man and how they might be of service here on this planet. It was his parable of the Moon Boots and the dead kid made wearable, a constant costume that summed up the cruelty, the creativity, and the continuation of the human condition.

．•．

After Banana shuttered down, we moved to a little arts-and-crafts house on Mulberry Street. It was 1973, and I'd just turned ten.

Thovas and I ping-ponged between Mom's enshrined sewing area inside the house and the detached garage that had become Preston's haven. Out there, he tinkered with cars and other spare handyman work—jobs he'd taken up to support the family. It was a back-and-forth between their respective realms, both busy and bright but, notably, separate. They'd collaborate at times—painting neon portraits over the fading floral wallpaper, giving input on one another's projects—but something had shifted.

Still, someone was usually always home. So when I rode up on my bike one evening to find all the lights off and no car in the driveway, I sensed something was off. There was a chemical smell in the air I'd never noticed before. Then I saw my father's white V-neck and 501s smoldering on the ground, slashed to bits. I threw down my bike and ran to the neighbor's, who could only communicate the words: *Father. Fire. Ambulance.*

Every bit of my skin went cold and hot; all I could do was sit down on the porch and wait and wait. It was way past sunset when Anna pulled into the driveway alone. She shared details about a carburetor exploding, hitting a cup of gasoline Dad had been holding. His face, head, neck, shoulder, right arm and hand were badly burned. I couldn't press her for more; I was so in shock. And anyway, she offered no comfort. She'd already gone into her room and shut the door. I lay awake, blinking until the sun rose, begging for it all to be false.

For some reason, Anna thought it would be a good idea for me to go to school that next day. Unbrushed, unwashed, unfed, and overwhelmed, I showed up; anxiety creeping over my skin in hives that mirrored Preston's burns. Day in and out, I existed like this, hardly sleeping, barely roused by my brother. At some point, I started crying and couldn't stop. My teacher finally called my mother. She'd never seen a kid this distraught—was there any way I could see my father? The doctor eventually gave in and would allow it, though he warned: *There are just some things a child shouldn't see.*

I'd seen so much, and I didn't understand, but then, I hadn't known what fire could do to a body or ever thought it could affect so many at one time, in one place.

The Brooke Army Hospital burn ward was one big open room lined with beds, and every single one was full. I was dizzy and scared; my eyes scanning all these bandaged figures, just hoping I would recognize my father at all. Finally, I spied the tattoo on his chest, a small homage to the duckling he'd found as a child, emblazoned over his heart. Then, his blue-eye beacons drew me to his side. *Your eyes are OK, so you're OK,* I told him, unsure of what to do with my own eyes and where to look. I settled on his hands—the unburned one, his left, opening to me.

∴

I sat there for hours that day, listening to Preston and watching him rest, meeting the men who surrounded him: men missing eyelids and noses, who put Dad's damage and my dog-attack scars all into perspective. In that shared purgatory, there were just as many words of support as there were cries of pain, sent and received energies of strength to and from people experiencing the same sort of untouchable torture. Everything was whittled down to the limits of what one could withstand. I went there every day for weeks.

They do this thing when you've been burned, put you in a tank full of disinfected water, and take a wire brush to all the dead skin. They scrub it all the way down to the blood, erasing every boundary. And the people just scream, and they're in agony. Once they started doing that to Dad, I wasn't allowed back.

Consciously or not, I decided that for as raw as my father's skin got, I'd pile on extra armor. I became a robot, a soldier: school, Thovas, home. Mom never spoke to us about Dad's accident, didn't sit us down at the dinner table, or cuddle on the couch to talk about our feelings. Anna had never been very affectionate or warm anyway, and now she was just absent. I guessed she was at the burn ward, but there's really no telling.

She did send a friend over to check on us—a woman who stopped by exactly twice, swooping in like she was making this big contribution. The first time this lady came, she slopped Chef Boyardee ravioli into a pot, plastered it with a pile of salt, clicked on the burner, and left. The next night, she returned, shaking a box of Kraft Mac n' Cheese like she was summoning feral cats. When we asked her to please not put so much salt this time, she turned and leveled us with angry eyes. *You little fucking ingrates!* she yelled and left.

Eventually, I quit school. I stayed home with Thovas, keeping the house spotless in case Anna came home, and drawing a million cards for my dad's impending return. When my father did arrive, it was like the sun on my face on those Triumph rides, like every warm and good thing you've ever known walking in your front door. I ran to him and hugged him as hard as I could, keeping in mind his burns. I read to him and kept his V-necks and hospital-issued pajama pants clean, cooked plates and plates of scrambled eggs.

Dad had a hard time using his right hand, but every single day, he fiddled in his sketchbook, trying to get it to work again. I watched his blurred, bandaged arm's every movement. He mainly sketched the large pecan tree outside the window with a slow-motion cross-hatch that echoed leaves in a breeze. My peace returned with each soft, smooth line, soothed by the scratching that, from the very beginning, was linked to my breath.

Each new layer of Dad's skin peeled, restitched, and warmed, and then again. The circular process of healing played out visually, viscerally: nonlinear, undefined as it refines. Painful but hopeful as a newborn baby.

∴

Preston's litany to me throughout the ordeal was that soon, all would be "back to normal." It was a sweet thing for a father to say, and I wanted to believe it more than anything but I also wasn't real sure what he meant. New normals just kept resurfacing in our lives, like a rearranged shore, wave after wave after wave. Still, I floated on his words, the sound of his sketching and painting. After a few weeks, he took up heavier tools; hammering and sawing resumed their background metronome.

The VA sent a social worker to help Dad rehabilitate. He was a pretty dull dude, so it was extra shocking when, one night, Anna summoned Dad to the porch to admit she and the social worker were having an affair; they were in love, and she wanted a divorce. Anna had screamed a lot of shit at Preston over the years, but she'd never said that.

Thovas and I stayed glued to the wall near the screen door, which slapped shut as Dad came in to gather some things—a few copies of his uniform, his sketchbook. He put them all in a duffel, walked around the garage, got on his bike, and rode away. My brother and I chased him to the end of the driveway, where he stopped and promised he'd be back. With a little wave, we watched his shape get smaller and smaller, listening as his bike chain whirr became a whisper. Another screen door slam signaled Anna's retreat to her bedroom. I scooped up my lanky little brother because I still could and lugged him inside. We fell asleep holding onto each other like we were all the other had in the whole world.

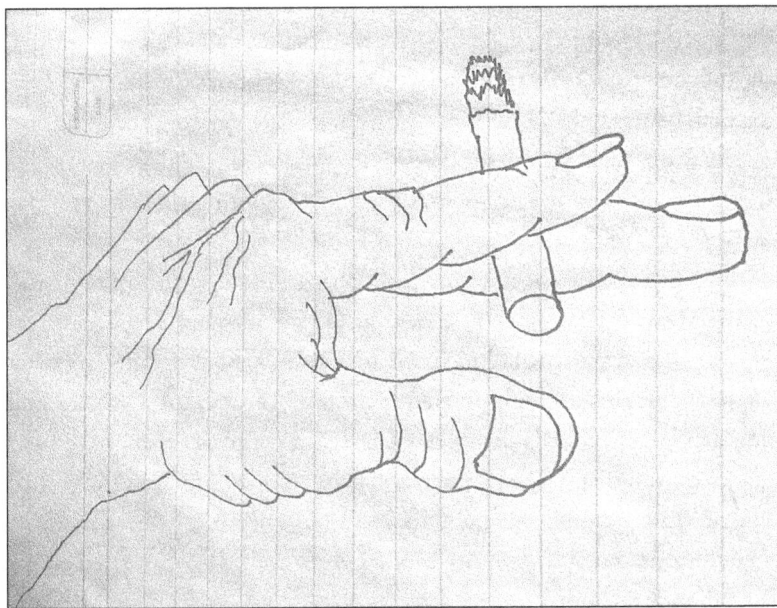

By Preston

⁖

The next day, I came home after school and found Anna chain-smoking on the porch. She didn't say a word but had a completely different look on her face that just chilled me right to the bone. This was something new, and I never figured out if it was an emergent alter or the chimera of alcoholism. 'Cuz Mom was drunker than I'd ever seen, and from that moment, we rarely ever saw her sober for very long, for decades. She was a whole new animal.

Alcohol was like lighter fluid on Anna. Everything immediately became beyond control; it even startled her, at least at first. Pretty quickly, Mom checked herself into the Villa Rosa mental hospital downtown to get sober. She stayed there for probably a month, and for that month, Thovas and I were left completely and totally alone for the very first time. There was no shitty friend who came to check on us with scoopfuls of sodium. We still had no reliable landline. Once we ran out of food, we took to living off pecans from the tree in the backyard and whatever else we could scavenge. The electricity got turned off and, eventually, the water did too.

It was old-school storybook fun for a minute, a mixture of trust and fear and a little mischief—Huckleberry Finn and a frolicking "fuck it." Thovas and I drank and took baths from our neighbor's garden hose, chasing each other down as we held our thumbs over the end, spinning arcs of sun-scattered rainbow droplets that we danced in. We could forage and filch sodas and sweets and ride our bicycles until sundown every day, forever—a world without end, Amen.

But I remember one unremarkable evening in those days of sameness and survival, watching my brother as he played out some real-life *Boxcar Children* scenario in the falling-down fort we'd slapped together out back. We were standing at the spot where I'd found Dad's clothes slashed and smoldering the day he'd caught fire, beneath the pecan tree that had fed and shaded us and that my father had drawn and redrawn to heal. I squeezed a giant Texas pecan in my palm like an overgrown prayer bead, a Shivalingam stone. I prayed that my brother and I would be protected—that even though we didn't know where our father was, how our mother was, or if we could or should contact our grandmothers, this tree that we could clearly see would sustain and shelter us through.

Just as a pecan is the fruit of the tree, it is also its seed. For a seed to grow, it has to obliterate itself completely. The boundaries of protection shatter as it turns inside out and goes underground. On that very day holding that pecan, something shifted within, clicked into place, and wrapped its wings around me. I was cocooned in survival mode, held in the faithful momentum.

Let my insides turn to mush; let me become something else, but let us stay safe.

⁘

And then one day, the sun rose and Mom came home. She just showed up sober and happy and calm. Sleepy, but not unkind. This lasted about a week.

At Villa Rosa, they'd given her heaps of pills but no tools to cope with the reality she was coming home to: her husband still gone and her kids in this limbo of wanting and needing her love and attention, but too afraid to ask or even hope for it. Thovas and I tiptoed around Anna's gentleness that first week, but the moment she started drinking again, it didn't matter what we said or did.

Thovas could do no wrong, but it was all I ever seemed to do. I don't remember a day going by then without a pretty harsh ass-whooping. Anna beat me with objects, with her hands, with whatever. I was turning eleven but had pretty much stopped functioning as a kid. I existed in a war zone, startling at every little thing. Life had gotten so surreal, and the only thing I knew to do was keep going.

As usual, just when shit was as fucked up as it could get, Anna decided to throw me a birthday party.

We were still at the house on Mulberry Street, though the eviction notices were piling up on the front porch like junk mail. A last hurrah in the backyard was all Mom cared about, her backward way of putting on a show as though she cared. She got drunk as a skunk and invited all the neighbors and my childhood friends from Banana Funk N' Junk. That lame old social worker was there casting his quiet, weird gloom.

It was the first birthday I spent without my father. I kept expecting him to show up with a little piece of cake with two lit number-one candles on top, dancing some silly chimney-sweep jig and singing Happy Birthday. I looked up at the pecan tree that was still dropping its fruit, and I knew Dad would want me to focus on that, to be patient, and to wait for him. I was grateful for the small break from the abuse that the party afforded me, thankful for my friends and the cake, but I missed my dad. And I was fucking tired of pecans.

∴

She'd put on a grand show for the party, but really, Mom had been getting sicker and sicker. I figured it was the booze, but Anna, the hypochondriac alcoholic that she was, insisted it was something more. And this time, she was right. Although she'd had her tubes tied after having Thovas, Mom just had this hunch she was pregnant. Clinic after clinic refused to even test her. By the time it was confirmed, it was too late for her to have an abortion. Somehow, Anna was gonna have another baby.

Everything went from shitty to straight to hell in seconds. Instead of seeing this child as a miracle of science and divine serendipity, Mom believed the baby was a bona fide curse. She set out to drink herself and the child to death immediately.

Anna started staying out all night again. She'd come home reeking and sleep the clock around, her belly rounder each return. If she were awake, she'd lash out at me for anything, then disappear again. The social worker visited her from time to time and holed up in her room. Then he just stopped showing up altogether.

I wasn't going to school. We got evicted. We moved. We probably migrated to about fifteen different residences in the months Mom was pregnant. Our belongings dwindled to nothing: the clothes on our backs, some blankets, and Great-Grandma Peggy's big bean pot. The places were never real far from each other—a carousel of roach-infested holes-in-the-wall around the Monte Vista neighborhood. Maybe Mom would pay the first month's rent to get us in a place, but we'd get kicked out once she drank away next month's money, splitting in the middle of the night on foot. Oftentimes, we kind of just squatted somewhere abandoned until we got found out.

As much as I tried to provide some sort of stability for my brother, all the little details floated around in the centrifugal spin. Trying to put the events of that time into a linear story is like describing the path of a tornado: a wider angle can show you the overall pattern, but the real story is on the ground, where the bits of everything that once made up your life are all shattered and scattered. Stunned, you shuffle through the debris, at a loss of how to make it beautiful again, amazed you survived at all.

I was tired and scared, but I was holding onto the hope that this new little baby would bring some much-needed joy to our family, some softness to the jagged edges of our home. Maybe *this* kid would be the one to snap Mom out of her stupor and set her on a sweeter path. I was a dreamer, and I just wanted to love.

∴

The pacts of children are holy little husks, the most well-intentioned things in the universe. Sealed with spit, whispered for safety, they're the things we're most afraid to speak and the covenants that keep this great world spinning.

Thovas and I made a deal—the first of many—to not tell anyone anything. It was too much pain to put on anyone, and we never wanted to bring trouble or have anyone feel burdened by a situation we thought we could handle. That's way too much responsibility for a kid, but we didn't know it then.

It's a sixth sense among abused and neglected children to protect your situation, no matter how awful. Like Mom's alters, our sense of protection was made up of beliefs and behaviors that seem at odds with what people in different circumstances might consider instinctual. We were beginning to get the hang of this fucked-up terrain, and Anna had made it clear that if we spoke to anyone, Thovas and I would be separated, and that was scarier than anything. We weren't to make a peep to neighbors or friends—and especially not to Dad—about Mom's stay at Villa Rosa. She was gonna beat me no matter what I did, but I couldn't lose my brother.

So, we stuck to our code of secrecy. The folks in our Monte Vista neighborhood knew our faces and our facts, but everyone had their own hard-scrabble bullshit to deal with. I'd do odd jobs cleaning or babysitting, telling my next-door employers I was saving up for some typical-kid thing: a twirling baton with ribbons, a new bike. They entertained my tale and paid what they could, maybe sneaking me a loaf of bread and a jar of peanut butter that fed Thovas and me for days.

That small sustenance was everything. Our neighbors understood the world was cruel and convoluted. The only way through was to help each other out however we could, not snitch on each other's situations, and pray through bits of beauty. Those streets my brother and I learned each inch of might've been rough, but woven into each block were bright murals, mosaics laid into the pavement, strings of music from front porches, and concrete Madonnas everywhere. Life still held magic, these instances urged. As long as I could hold my brother's hand, I knew it to be true.

∴

In the course of all this desperate momentum, Preston sought us out, spotted Thovas and me on a walk, and stopped. He hugged us tight, told us where to find him, and then rode off. From that moment, we snuck to see him every chance we got.

Mom had spies everywhere, and each visit risked a pretty serious beatdown for me, but I figured it was worth it. Thovas would prop his little butt on the handlebars of whatever bike I could find and we'd circus-cycle our way to Dad. He lived in a space he'd named The Refinery: a half head shop/half apartment where he sold bongs and one-hitters, used records, and black light posters to college kids. He taught art to people from the neighborhood in the front and slept in the back.

Preston had taken the months alone, away from us, to sit in his pain.

Deep meditations and massive amounts of Vitamin E had redefined him entirely: instead of lumpy scars, the remnants of the fire surfaced as pale pinkish birthmarks, brand-new baby smooth. His rough, old left hand was work-weathered, but his right hand was shiny and soft, always forever warm and without a trace of fingerprints. I'd sit and hold and look at them, turning them over in my own hands, dirty paws at the ends of scarred arms. My eyes blurred to look at our hands together, tears plunking on our grubby puddle of knuckles. It was so fucking sad and held every hope I ever had.

No topic was off-limits for me and him except for the one that was most pertinent and vulnerable and scary. I couldn't tell him exactly what was happening. Beneath Preston's reborn skin, I sensed his anger bubbling close to the surface, searing. I feared he'd fly apart at the seams if I said a word about it. So, instead, we'd talk about God and Buddha and Jesus and Bob Dylan and The Rolling Stones, Vincent van Gogh and Sitting Bull and Annie Oakley. He expressed how frustrated he was at no longer being able to cut his hair, which grew thin and sparse as new shoots now, where it grew at all.

∴

Then, in no time at all, there was this baby.

The day Amy was born, in July of 1976, Preston came to the hospital. The deadbeat social worker sure wasn't stepping up to the plate in any capacity. Dad saw Amy as an innocent child who was gonna be part of his children's lives and who wasn't to blame for anything. He claimed my little sister, and she became a Brown. We three siblings could share the same last name, at least. It was one of those tender moments in life where messy grown-ups do one clean thing. And for maybe that single moment Mom thought Amy was a blessing. But for about a thousand reasons, Dad couldn't stay. His last name was all he had to give.

As Preston left the hospital, Mom's heart shut down further, shameful for hope. You could almost hear the clang of its iron gates, the drawbridge cranking shut as she looked over at my little sister, scrawny and screaming in her little bassinet. Amy represented to Anna the embodiment of all she had feared since the tube came untied: a real and true hex.

Amy was a biological wonder, but what was really birthed that day was something else.

Any rage Mom had displayed up to that point was just a holiday sparkler my young eyes had mistaken for a blaze. Scorned and worn out, mis- and undiagnosed with nearly every psychological condition you can imagine, Anna picked up the shards of what we had before called broken and spit them like nails.

Mom brought Amy home from the hospital, handed her to me, and left. There were no explanations given, and none asked for. Just chaos. Then silence. Then wailing.

Everything that was just barely held together now completely turned to shit.

Babies pin you to the moment, to the immediate. In an instant, mine and Thovas's childhood was taken away, but there was no time to feel bad about it.

I fell madly in love with Amy, and I was terrified. I've never seen a baby so thin: malnourished, Fetal Alcohol Syndrome, detoxing. She was bald as a cue ball, and oh my God, she never stopped crying. But I thought she was the cutest thing in the whole world.

Her need hit me like a punch in the solar plexus. I clasped one hand around both of her feet and started rubbing as I stared into her wide-open, freaking-out baby eyes. It wasn't just a basic insecurity I saw but also the deep sadness of our mother. She was her spitting image. I held her so tight.

∴

There was never any way of knowing where or when Anna would show up.

Sometimes, she'd leave to return the very next day; sometimes, it was weeks later. She had a little powder-blue vintage suitcase she'd throw costume jewelry into, a bottle of jungle gardenia perfume, and a few slips and shoes. Sometimes, she came back carrying it, sometimes not. When the welfare check arrived, she'd appear only to cash it, spend it on alcohol, and disappear again.

I knew some of Mom's haunts from years of mentally collecting the names of drinking holes my grandmother Louise had pointed out on random drives. From snippets of conversations and found matchbooks. Forever an anxious Nancy Drew, I was a hyper-alert twelve-year-old super-sleuth piecing together clues about my mother's life.

I kept my ears and eyes open. *Where was she?*

And my heart cautiously ajar: *Is she OK? Can we see her?*

Things had to get real bad before I went to find her—food stamps and formula run out, power and water cut. I'd venture out, alone or with my siblings in tow, Amy tied to me with a long scarf and Thovas scuffling along behind. Country bars, *conjunto* bars, gay bars, and biker bars, black bars, white bars—I knew 'em all, and they knew the looks of me, Amy, and Thovas. We'd throw open the door, two back-lit scrawny angels carting around this forever-crying creature, offending everyone inside with the bold announcement of daylight.

When Mom drank close to home, it was at a beer joint on Main called Buddy's Ice Box. The owners were two old gay men who had frequented Banana Funk N' Junk. Anna felt a comfort there among the familiar fixtures that had passed through her hands, a tiny measure of serenity in the company of kind men who wanted nothing from her. It was her honky-tonk reprieve, where she sat and drank beer after beer in front of the old jukebox, a bowl of quarters in her lap, pressing hard those acrylic buttons that held the combination to her heart.

She played George Jones's "He Stopped Loving Her Today" so many times she wore the poor record out. He and Hank Williams were Mom's soul brothers who could sing all she couldn't say. They each had that weathered old, lovesick carnie-Dad spirit she understood. Things were OK when she was at Buddy's, safe and surrounded by angels who helped me pry her off that barstool and bring her back home.

Sometimes, we'd discover our mother in the middle of some fun, dancing and laughing and carrying on. Sometimes, she was passed out, her head in her arms on the bartop or curled up in the alley. Always, her make-up was smeared down her face from sweating and crying, her clothes crumpled and cigarette-reeking, and always I'd get a slap, no matter her state.

I'd tug at her elbow or shake her real lightly and summon her to wherever we might've called home at the moment.

∴

One time, all my detective work failed: between ten and twenty bars, I rode miles on my bicycle, just circling. I'd left Thovas and Amy in front of some neighbor's TV after the usual places came up Mom-less. It wasn't the first or last time I figured Anna for dead, but that didn't make things any easier.

Downtown near the Bexar County Jail was a detox center Mom had once told me about. It was worth a try. The guard on duty was all business, but he had a little mercy. A woman had just come in, he said, a bit rowdy. He led me down a hallway that smelled of puke and bleach to a heavy metal door with a slot in the middle I could peek through.

It was a glimpse into my worst nightmare, a dimly lit padded cell where I saw Anna hunched in a corner, dressed in a tight white coat, her arms strapped around her resting form. There were spots of vomit all over the front, smeared and smelling. She had no shoes. I asked the guard what the straitjacket was for, and he said it was so she didn't hurt herself.

The sound of my voice woke up my mother, who began screaming my name over and over. *Get me out of here!* she pleaded. The guard slid shut the scrap of metal over the slot, but I could still hear Mom's voice all the way down the hall as he rushed me out the front door. I climbed on my bicycle with shaking legs and sweaty palms. Tears and snot gummed up my sight and my breath as I struggled to get away. After about a block, I pulled over and threw myself to my knees, puking and bawling and punching the ground.

When I got back to my siblings, Thovas asked about Mom. It was the only time I ever lied to him. We fell asleep as we did each night, arms and legs entwined, tight as that straitjacket.

∴

The same material used for straitjackets is used for sails, for paintings, and skate shoes. What holds us down might set us free if only we can see.

Sometimes in our lives, we can't dedicate a space or even a time to formally create anything. The ground is part of the medium, and it all spins. It's hard to see what is being built when you're in the middle of chaos. Sometimes, the evidence is all we have. I learned to allow whatever marks the world made to speak their space, and I drew around them what I could.

Creativity promises you a mess; making meaning of that mess is the whole world. Sometimes, it's all chaos, a collection of stains. Art is just an offering to the process. Burns and beatings refine; it is up to us, as we heal and create, to redefine.

My father's white V-necks were never really white; they were forever covered in paint splats and coffee spills. My mother's garb bore the stains and rips of her personal hurricane. When I couldn't see him or focus on her, I thought of these small details. The clothes I create today often carry these scars: doodles and fallen flecks, stabs at understanding, interpreting.

Shrouds of survival.

Chapter 6

WEAR YOUR
REVOLUTION

AFTER ANNA'S STINT AT THE MENTAL FACILITY, MY GRAND-
mother Louise started showing up.

At first, it was only on Saturdays when she'd bring Thovas a steak and
the rest of us a half-dozen glazed chocolate donuts from this one bakery
on San Antonio's East Side. The treats were so greasy you'd have to lick
the roof of your mouth for hours to get the glaze off. We gobbled them
up, starving and smacking. Amy would sit there in her big cloth diaper
with chocolate icing smeared all over everything, happy with her sugary
pacifier for a bit.

Those were Louise's only donations to our cause, not that we dared
ask her for anything. If she noticed the cupboards were bare, as they were
perpetually, you could almost see a sniff of tenderness breeze across her—
Catholic guilt mixed with a basic compassion that for a minute saw us as
innocent children in need. But just as quick, it dwindled. She'd visibly
shake it off and sit up straight, announcing, well, she'd be sure to stop and
light candles for us at church on her way home.

A whole trail of votives she must've lit, and I don't think they did shit.

∴

As Amy grew bigger, Anna grew worse and worse. When she returned home, it was at odd hours. We'd find her collapsed on the floor, often in a pool of vomit, in a dead-weight coma for days. I'd clean up the puke and throw a blanket on top of her, and we'd all try to stay out of the house as much as possible. Often, when we returned, she'd just be gone again, but when she did stick around, she was often in the bathroom, violently ill.

Mom's alcoholism had gotten so advanced that drying out on her own was dangerous, the withdrawals wreaking havoc on her whole system. She'd been taking pills, too, and God knows what else. If it got too bad, which was all the time, Anna went to a detox center, a rehab, a mental institution. Anywhere that would take her. So even when she was "home," Mom was still often away, trying to sober up.

She'd succeed for a week or two or three at most, and, in those stretches, Louise showed up all the time. On the surface, she was there to help Mom get on her feet, to take her to doctor's appointments and such. Louise still had her antiques store and would rouse Mom to open another shop. And in Mom's short sober stints, amazingly, she would.

They'd drive around in Louise's old beater, chain-smoking as they visited estate sales and auctions, yard sales, and thrift stores. They'd even go down to the Rio Grande Valley to shop the *ropas usadas*, massive warehouses strung along the border stacked to the ceiling with used clothing. Waist-deep hills of old fabrics sold by the pound rose from bare concrete floors, each item worn, passed over, and handed down a thousand times. For Anna, it was like piles of gold. She waded into that sea of texture and color like a natural baptism, her honed eyes and sure hands selecting the finest fabrics as though by instinct, guided by the highest good her soul had retained.

Back home, Mom immediately got to work ripping and shredding each piece, mixing and reassembling them. She *had* to get to the essence of the thing—to feel with her hands the undoing and watch with her own eyes the reconnection. The ensembles she created had never been seen before or since.

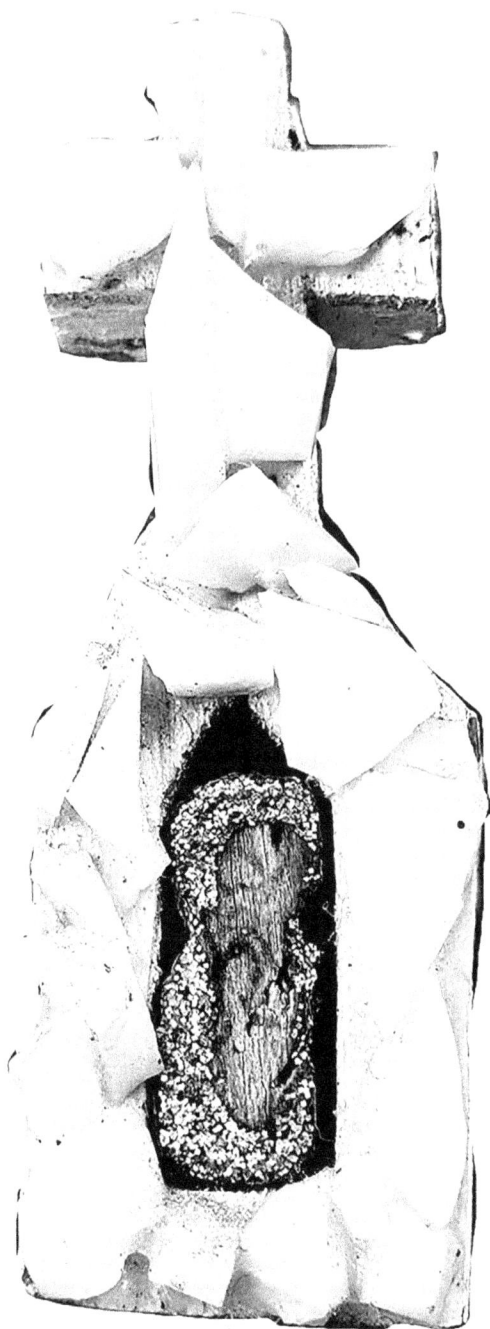

By Anna

Sometimes, they floated us. Powered by the mania of sheer creation, Mom might cobble together a little collection of clothing, set up shop in some shabby space in town, and keep it going until the owner demanded rent. When she got kicked out, as she always did, then she'd sell the rest of the pieces from wherever we lived.

Louise would come over, then, with an ice-cold six-pack of Tecate. They'd share a beer, which became many beers, the *CLICK-HISS!* of those bright red cans and their iconic eagle symbol signaling chaos. It was a sickness my matriarchal line couldn't shake: if Louise kept Anna down and drunk, my mom needed her.

They were addicted to each other, caught in a cycle of pain they couldn't outright acknowledge and, therefore, couldn't heal. The textiles and Tecates were stand-ins for the unspeakable. These women were both so capable and so vulnerable. It all hurt too much, and that hurt had to go somewhere.

⋖⋗

Mom wasn't someone who'd beat on you and be done in a few minutes. Often, it was a crazy-ass marathon of hitting and scratching and hair-pulling as she yelled the most vile things I'd ever heard. How she hated me and wanted me to die. I was a worthless piece of trash, the worst thing that had ever happened to her. How she wanted to kill me.

I was too stubborn or prideful, but I wasn't gonna beg her. I wasn't even gonna let her know she was getting to me. I'd roll up in a little ball and drift away to a place I made in my head, this serene dreamscape whose details became more intricate and real with each episode. I lived there just as much as I did all the falling-apart rooms we occupied then.

Like the kind on meditation tapes, I'd hear this voice beckoning and calming me. A soft female voice angelically negated each of Anna's curses, guiding me to a green landscape with statues, sloping paths, and quaint footbridges, the lip of the Japanese sunken gardens in San Antonio. Each paint-by-number scale of the koi fish in the ponds, the flat planes of the lily pads' deep green, the feel of a breeze and the sun on my skin—every detail pulling me away from pain and terror, soothing me in a synesthesia whose colors I could hear.

I never fought back, not once, and I know Mom probably wanted me to. But I remember thinking, *Fuck that!* It was stubbornness and, somewhat paradoxically, respect. It was self-preservation. Nothing I could do would stop her, so I just endured. As I walked through those gardens in my mind, I tuned a mantra to the rhythmic pulse of the waterfall I'd envisioned, syncopated with Anna's strikes, *It's not her fault. It's not her fault. It's not her fault.*

I knew she had to be suffering beyond human comprehension. I couldn't reach out to her, but I could keep steady. I could become a roly-poly and let it resolve itself however it was meant to.

Dents in my shin bones to this day bring back the time she wielded an iron skillet as a weapon, bashing it against my legs over and over. For weeks, I couldn't pull up my socks or wear long pants to cover them; they were so tender and exposed.

These, and others, the tally marks upon my bones.

∴

The experience of trauma sinks into our creature cells, where logic and reason take a backseat to our psyche. There it festers, paralyzed, waiting in the dark like a neglected and starving child until you gently tend to it. Someday, it begins to howl.

Around the time I turned thirteen, in 1976, I started getting migraines. My body was growing, going through hormonal changes, and undergoing the strain of physical abuse and the weight of carting two siblings around. Plus, I wasn't sleeping. I was malnourished and perpetually stressed.

I thought this was a normal part of being a human: people's necks always hurt. But these aches came with near-constant nausea and ice-pick stabs from one eye to the back of the skull, the inability to eat or drink.

If I made even a peep to Anna about having a headache, she'd just hit me harder and load on more work. I learned fast to button my lip and soldier on, but, somehow or another, Louise discovered my malady and, lo-and-behold, took me to a doctor. She loved doctors more than anything, just like Mom did. They both relished being bona fide sick and having something solid to explain away their behavior.

Louise drove me downtown to the nicest place I'd ever been inside of, a chiropractor's office in a historical home with oak wood paneling and plush carpet. There, she played the saint: the concerned, benevolent grandmother who'd do anything to help. She loved that shit and her role in this clandestine bit of charity. I laid on the table and got pushed and pulled and cracked, given shots of B12 in my bony backside. I don't remember anyone at the office making a peep about any of my bruises or scars, and if they did, I'm sure I told them I fell off my bicycle or had been wrestling with my brother.

It felt so good to be cared for, even if it was just a Band-Aid. But those visits were all part of my grandmother's sophisticated brand of fuckery.

The codependent cycle of harm was something Louise was subconsciously desperate to hand down to me—withholding care and pretending attention. She was chomping at the bit for the moment I'd call in sick with Anna and succumb to it. When that didn't happen to her liking, the pressure crept from her nervous system to her hands, and she began beating me, too.

∴

A filched pocket watch had gotten my grandmother blocked from the estate sale circuit, which was a tight-knit bunch. Word spread like wildfire in that hallowed community. Cut off from the lifeblood that lined her shelves, she needed an in. Again, a kid is a key.

Scouting for Banana Funk N' Junk and the hours spent in carsick backseat rides with Mom and Louise, the few times they could see some use for my company, had sharpened my antiquing eye. Louise sent me into the field as her proxy, picking, haggling, and seeking. She was using me, but it was good to feel useful for something other than survival. And it was fun.

She'd told me to seek out old religious artifacts; the heavier, the better. What I couldn't find or carry, she outsourced to a Cadillac full of dudes who pillaged cemeteries in exchange for a case of beer. I stood with Louise one day as the men unloaded the loot—kneeling angels and engraved crosses, all encrusted with fresh dirt. She'd promised me she never got these relics from actual burial plots; when I dared point out the evidence to the contrary, Louise wheeled around and backhanded me in the face. I fell on my ass and held my cheek as she pointed her finger in my face. *Shut your mouth and mind your own fucking business*, she snarled. The family credo that had kept so much buried for so long.

Weeks later, Louise picked a fight with me on one of her steak, donut, and Tecate drop-offs. She was wasted to the heavens and furious as hell about who knows what. She was expecting Anna, but I'd have to do. Yelling escalated to shoving, and the second she grabbed a hammer, I took off like a shot.

I pounded up the stairs to our shared bathroom and barricaded myself behind the paper-thin veneer door, which was no match for the claw end of the hammer. I flung myself at the itty-bitty window above the toilet, pulling with all my might at its pane. Louise made quick work of that door, and soon she was on me with the hammer, hacking away at my back. She got a few good jabs in before I could wrestle her weapon away from her and smash it through the window, which refused to open. As I leaned over the sill, fragments of glass piercing my palms, I saw a cyclone of dogs below me. Hopped up by the commotion and mangy-mad, they circled, baring their teeth and barking. I had a choice between my murderous grandma and a pack of ferocious beasts, so I said a little prayer and launched myself out, kicking away at Louise's clawing grasp.

I landed smack on a hurricane fence, whose little top barbs gouged my arms but saved me from the dogs' jaws, snapping at the hems of my jeans. Pure adrenaline got me to an old Funk N' Junk friend's house. Her mother dressed my wounds and fed me a little orange pill in the shape of a house. In shock, sedated, I slept until the middle of the next day.

∴

Neither Mom nor Louise ever once struck my brother or sister. In a way that's only so typical of siblings in any situation, Thovas and Amy wondered what I'd done to make them so mad that they had to beat me. As far as Anna went, there was no way for me *not to* provoke her, but I figured I could bear her wrath if it meant they didn't have to.

A twisted sense of normalcy settled in around these frequent traumas. We had no vocabulary for what was happening or context for what a healthy dynamic might be. As these instances of violence occurred, Thovas would run and hide, and Amy would cry. When Anna had her fill, she'd stop cold and go to her room if she had one, shut the door, and blare the TV or sleep. Usually, she just left and never said anything further about it.

Sometimes, I'd go off and cry for a minute to release the tension, but I tried hard not to. I never wanted my brother or sister to see me crying. But I'd have lumps all over. Patches of my hair would be ripped out. Scratched and black and blue. Thovas would come out of his hiding place and Amy would toddle to my side, and we'd shiver together until we all fell asleep.

The code of silence that insulated us also isolated us from each other, even as we huddled together. Around that time, though, things began to happen that put a question in my siblings' minds, a suspicion that Mom's behavior was, at the very least, different.

∴

We were on welfare and could go to a doctor if we needed to, but Mom never took us. If we needed dental work—which we always did, never having toothbrushes and living on donuts—we rode the bus by ourselves to the dentist's office and back, all numb and drooly and unsupervised.

But if Mom was home, she was *always* going to see a doctor. On top of everything else, Anna perpetually thought she was dying of cancer. That was her big thing. Anytime she got an ache or an itch anywhere on her body, she was 100 percent sure it was The End. If she couldn't make it to a doctor immediately, she invited us kids into her madness, a front-row seat to things children should never have to see. No body part was off-limits for Anna to fully display to us for examination—mirrors, flashlights, and commands we scan for any suspicious sore or lump.

If for one moment we hesitated to respond that everything appeared healthy, she panicked. We learned quickly to dance the dance that kept her comfortable and kept her from twisting off. We soothed her insanity for our survival.

Thovas was about seven years old then, and Mom's constant insistence on inspecting her body messed with him. Mom had always favored Thovas in her way. She hugged him, and they could carry on some kind of conversation. She'd cook him spaghetti. But when all this bizarre shit began, Thovas started to shut down around Mom. He wouldn't go to her as much, or at all. His hands shook. He became overly interested in fire.

I kept my brother close. He started missing a lot of school. He was so young, and I didn't task him with helping me much, but he was glued to my side.

∴

Mom filed a peace bond against Preston at some point in the mayhem. To my knowledge, he hadn't done anything threatening to her, but once Mom discovered that Dad was settling down with a new lady, she had it *out* for him. The peace bond effectively forbade us from seeing each other, an efficient way of hurting all of us at the same time. She knew we were all so madly in love.

Dad fought for custody of us over the years, many times, and never won. Even though she didn't take care of us, even though she beat me every chance she got, Anna wanted custody. And, amazingly, she got it. If Preston had custody of us, Mom would've lost the check she relied on to drink and lost her babysitters and housekeepers. She needed someone to take care of Amy full-time.

And she hated being alone.

The winds blew in a string of awful men who appeared on our couch or materialized from Mom's rooms, each different but the same. A few were just friends, fellow alcoholics, and addicts Anna had met on the street or out at bars who needed a place to stay. Some she dated, many she married. Mom never legally divorced anyone except my father. She'd just go downtown and keep changing her name over and over.

These guys would live with us for a week or two or a year. A few were OK; some struck out at us kids with their words and their fists. And a few were actual monsters.

∴

Jim was one of the worst. He was a roughneck roofer with a taste for alcohol, and he and Mom were inseparable, synced up in their cycles, matched in their manias, toe-to-toe in their addictions and afflictions. They'd stumble home late from the bars, fall all over the place, and get down to their grown-up business right there on the floor in front of where we kids slept. I'd cover Thovas and Amy with pillows and blankets, shoving my fingers in my ears and squeezing my eyes shut.

Amy was still in diapers but talking a little. I spoke her language, but she began to babble strange things about Jim. I was confused. Droplets of blood in the crotch of her cloth diapers punctuated the sentences I couldn't believe she was speaking. My instinct said to tell Anna. That surely *this* would be the last straw that would get her to stand up for her children.

By that point, I should've known better.

About a year before Jim came into our lives, Mom had let a male friend stay with us, a jewelry designer and an animal lover, a non-drinker. I thought he was cool. He taught me how to make jewelry and gave me rides in his pickup. He was my friend, or so I thought. One night, I dreamt someone's hands were fumbling around in my underpants. I woke up to find him standing there.

Even in the middle of the night, woken from sleep, violated, my first thought was shame-flavored: *What had I done to make him put his hands on me? Had I given him the wrong impression?* After that moment of fright, of freeze, came fight. Right at that moment, I looked this man square in the eye, and he backed off. He left the following day, and we never saw him again.

I learned to go without sleep to protect my siblings from this bullshit. I was hyper-vigilant, but I wasn't superhuman. I never mentioned to Mom anything about my assault, but I couldn't bear the same thing happening to Amy.

When I told Anna about finding the blood in the diaper, she beat me and beat me. Louise had never stood up for Anna throughout all those years of sexual abuse, and because her own mother had never once protected her, it was now my role to absorb Anna's anger and disappointment about it.

Jim stayed.

∴

Often, we can't break a cycle for ourselves. When our survival depends upon silence, we sometimes forget the words and gestures necessary to make a change. It can take something we can't stand happening to someone else, someone we love who's usually younger than us, to flip on the light in that room in our minds, illuminating clearly what needs to happen.

The long, lumpy rectangles of cotton diapers we got in stacks from churches served as more for me than repositories for my sister's toileting and trauma. At some point, while folding their never-ending stacks, I thought to stitch a few together into a *huipil*. The simply constructed, elemental garment of women in Mexico, Guatemala, and beyond, *huipiles* had always been Anna's fashion staples, made and found.

I hand-sewed a few together into a larger rectangle with armholes and an opening to fit my head through. I embroidered flowers and planets upon them and wore these creations to shreds. They were the perfect shifts for riding around with my siblings, soaking up all our sweat and tears.

∴

My mother always found huge batches of Victorian clothes on her thrift hauls. No one ever wanted these old rags mended and patched to their last breath. In Victorian times, when garments were passed on, they could easily be made smaller, but it wasn't so simple to make them bigger. Increasing fabric suggests abundance, a right to thrive. Women of that time were expected to stay as small and quiet as possible; many pieces from this period look like they'd only fit a hungry child.

Magnolia Pearl started with these pieces: bloomers, chemises, pantaloons, and slips cut for an adult. So many people laughed at me, but I didn't care. The people these creations spoke to understood their small power and soft rebellion.

Revolutions begin with what is most intimate, with the things against our skin. Clothing creators the world over and throughout time have taken the greatest risks expressing themselves through what is hidden—reimagining movement and finding breath.

The alterations reverberate through each successive layer.

So much of life belongs
to our hands.
We hold hands, we shake hands,
we make food, we paint,
we open doors, we write,
we weave threads.
We plant, we pull, we push,
we build, we touch, we weave.
Close your eyes. Put your hand to
your heart.
The meeting point between the two
is the beginning of grace.

Chapter 7

PATCHING

THEY SAY IF YOU'RE STANDING AT THE EDGE OF A VOLCANO
when it erupts, stare right down into the cauldron and then look up into
the sky. That way, you can trace the trail of the firebombs raining down
and possibly avoid them.

As the revolving door of shitty men kept spitting out even worse versions of the one before, there was no way to sidestep the insanity. Some
alter of Anna's resonated with these men's darkness of spirit, forming an
awful cloud of pure evil that consumed everything.

Each day was a tightrope walk over a volcano. I couldn't see the next
step, couldn't see the other side. My siblings were the two ends of my
balancing pole. It was one foot in front of the other atop a cauldron
that threatened to erupt at any moment. Every element challenged my
equilibrium.

Often, I fell right into the flames, burned alive, it felt like. I'd come to
in a heap on the bathroom floor, begging God or Mary or the Universe
or something, *anything*, for some mercy. Just a little bit.

There was no voice, no one came, but a stillness would fill me—a presence, a breath as small as the first ones I ever took—that gave me just
enough lift to carry on.

∴

Starting when I was eleven or twelve years old, Dad would take me down to the headwaters of the San Antonio River at the Incarnate Word Academy for an exercise he called "Fire and Ice."

There's this wishing-well kind of monument called "The Blue Hole," which is the river's source. It's deep and clear and shiny, and from there, it all flows. That was the starting point. We'd lean over the circle of rock and look right into the heart. Then, my father would walk, following the river's winding path to the missions downtown. And I, in turn, followed him.

It was many miles until sundown. We were both barefoot. It was just us: no siblings, no Anna—just one another and our naked feet. Certain parts of the journey were grassy and soft, the river flowing so sweetly beside. Other sections cut jagged paths beneath highway overpasses through littered homeless camps. The river there mucked up and stank. Slivers of broken glass stung my soles.

This was the Fire.

The Ice came at sunset, when we jumped into the river.

I know it sounds terrible. It sounds like child abuse. Fire and Ice was a kind of ancient ritual performed smack in the middle of a cityscape—both fully within the scene and entirely beneath it. It seemed like a dad and a kid going for a stroll until you looked closer, but no one ever did. I see children now and can't imagine their parents putting them through that, much less the kids going along with it. You might say it could give a kid PTSD or at least a different toehold on reality, and in some ways, it may have.

Preston knew that because of his addiction, he was constantly walking the razor's edge between life and death. He didn't hide this from me; his lessons were meant to steady me for that inevitable slip. And I just carried that with me, always. Like a gnawing pain in my heart. Waiting for the other shoe to drop.

Preston's palms upon my feet had woken me up as a baby. And he wanted me to stay awake.

He didn't want to shield me from the pains of the planet, and he knew he couldn't. It just wasn't possible. Dad knew my home life with Anna then was much the same, at least physically, as living under the bridge in those homeless camps. Limping around shattered glass was the same as tiptoeing through our living room. He didn't want me to walk blindly, but to walk with purpose. Even if that meant my feet got cut. Some way or another, your feet *will* get cut. You can't control that path.

If you get too comfortable in this life, he said, *you'll fall back asleep.* And then what would be the point? What use would you be? You must have character before comfort so you can always be alert, awake, alive. Doing something—that's the thing that creates passion.

It's comfortable to be asleep. Being awake is exhausting. Most people just shut their minds down because they don't want that exhaustion. They can't simply sit with discomfort, much less walk hand-in-hand with suffering. They only want the soothe.

I get it. So well.

As much as my bloody little feet cried for the river, my tired little soul often screamed for release. It felt too high a price to pay. Sometimes it still does, my eyes squeezed shut against the harsh light of day.

Just keep going.

∴

Amy had been born the summer between my sixth- and seventh-grade years. I'd tried to keep up attendance in middle school, at least at first—a present body with an exhausted soul, praying without ceasing for my family.

My sixth-grade teacher, Ms. Taylor, had been kind to me. A sweet spirit who didn't push too hard or pry too much, Ms. Taylor had allowed me to spend most of my sporadic attendance taking care of our class pets, two little gerbils. At the end of the school year, she asked if I wanted to take the gerbils home.

Thovas and I easily kept their little cage tidy, but cleaning had become this guillotine that hung over my head. Never knowing when Mom might barge in meant I had to keep wherever we lived completely spotless at all times. It could be a total shithole, infested with roaches, but if there was a speck of dust on the furniture, my ass was grass.

After tucking in the kids and feeding the gerbils, I was cleaning the kitchen when Mom walked in dead drunk. I'd left a single fork in the sink, and Anna lost her mind. In a blind rage and at close range, she hurled that fork right at my head, where it stuck. I reached up and felt this strange appendage to my skull as trickles of blood ran rivers down my face and neck. Through the shock, I felt the vibrations of Anna's stomping feet headed to where Amy and Thovas were sleeping. Then, there was a loud crash, followed by my siblings' wails.

Anna had chunked the gerbils' cage across the room so hard that it busted. The gerbils lay there dead. The scene was bizarre and beyond fucked up: I stood there with a fork sticking out of my skull, blood splattered everywhere, two dead gerbils, and two screaming kids.

Mom turned on her heel without a word, slammed her bedroom door, and passed out.

Thovas and I wrapped up the gerbils and dug a little grave for them in the alleyway behind our house. I blanketed my head in a towel and then collapsed in a heap, snuggled between my siblings, syncing our breaths to sleep.

⁙

When I saw Ms. Taylor at school that next year and she asked how the gerbils were doing, of course, I couldn't tell her. It was a terrible start to my seventh-grade year, and it didn't get much better. By the time I reached eighth grade, my classmates had voted me the ugliest kid in school, and my homeroom teacher, Ms. Cortez, announced in front of everyone that I was the least likely to succeed of any kid she'd ever taught. I failed most of eighth grade and had to attend summer school.

The teacher there allowed me to bring Amy and Thovas along. I'd pack some random toys, coloring books, and whatever blanket I could find, and they'd sit in the back of the class. After school, we grabbed fistfuls of donuts from the cafeteria and hoofed it back home.

Everything a parent would do for a child I did for Thovas and Amy. Keeping them grounded and fed and safe and happy as possible consumed every minute of my life for a few years.

We'd lug our laundry down to the laundromat together and back, come home, and I'd fold it and put it away while they played. Meals were whatever resourceful shit I could cobble together: lots of Top Ramen, peanut butter on day-old bread, and tortillas that we scraped the mold off of. Thovas's favorite creation of mine was a plate of cottage cheese with grated government cheese on top and whatever kinds of seeds or nuts we could find on top of that. Amy lived on bean and cheese tacos.

We weren't allowed to touch Anna's food, but Thovas once wanted chocolate milk so bad I mixed cocoa powder with Mom's precious buttermilk. I'll never forget the look on his face or the beating I received afterward once Anna realized I'd dipped into her stash.

There were snippets of light: watching *Mork & Mindy* and *Gilligan's Island* on TV if we had one—bike tricks and rounds of jacks, stacks of old magazines to cut up for collages. I tried to make games out of things as much as possible, and I hugged and kissed and held my brother and sister every chance I got.

And there was always music, and friends who were family. Those Banana Funk N' Junk kids and I had stayed close, a flock of black sheep, shit-deep scoundrels who knew how much we needed each other. Our bonds were forged from survival, reciprocal. Simple kindnesses and life-saving laughter. The family you choose may not be blood, but they're the ones who will help you mop it all up.

At night, Thovas, Amy, and I would crawl into whatever bed we all shared; I'd read them Shel Silverstein's *The Giving Tree* or whatever forever-overdue library books Thovas had picked out. I collected those little music magazines they used to sell at the checkout whenever I had a spare dollar. I'd read to my siblings the doings of Fleetwood Mac or Black Sabbath like they were myths. I'd sing them some Neil Young tune, and they'd drift off just glued to me. My tired body would struggle to find sleep amidst their tangled arms and night child breath, and it was worth it all.

By Anna

∴

But I was a child, too, and afraid of the dark, of night, of being alone, of starving. I hid those fears as best as I could, pretending, just to get on the other side of this. But the beasts of a child's nightmare—the ones that send you running to your parents' bed, suspicious of every shadow and sure of every dreaded demon—were real and near.

It didn't take long for child predators to learn there were three children living alone together.

We had the same mailman for years in that neighborhood. He seemed fine until he started trying to break into our house. With each overdue bill delivered, he'd fiddle with the latches on our window screens or jiggle the front door handle. We were terrified of him.

I cleaned this neighborhood guy's house for ten bucks a pop. The whole time I'd work, he did weird shit, walking around naked and stuff. With the money, I'd grab Thovas a pork chop, some milk and cereal, and a little box of Jiffy muffin mix. One night, our neighbor—this eccentric musician who had a demented Great Dane that was always running headfirst into vans in the neighborhood, denting them with his massive skull—broke into our house and stole our food. I heard him rustling around in the kitchen and ran after him, but he was gone.

A car full of men took to parking outside of the homes where we lived, sleeping in the car overnight and leering at us when we left, slowly shadowing our terrified footsteps and then speeding off.

∴

Around then, a little white kitty crossed our path.

She was just a fluff ball, patient, sweet, and in love with Amy, who had named her Crystal. The cat followed Amy everywhere, a gleaming shepherd that fussed over my baby sister and let Amy carry her all clumsy like a rag doll. We three doted on that cat like the Princess of Persia herself; she slept entwined with us at night, purring and warming us.

We needed that sweetness more than anything, and when Crystal went missing, we were distraught. We assumed she'd been hit by a car; she certainly wouldn't run off. Amy especially was heartbroken, so I tried to distract her. I'd bought her this box for fifty cents at a yard sale—a square blue vinyl case that looked like it was for carting records around, but it had ballerinas on the front, with compartments for toe shoes and tutus. It opened and closed like a cake box, with a snap at the top. I thought we could play ballerina, but the hasp at the top was stuck, and something stunk. In terror, I turned the latch, and sure enough, stuffed inside was little Crystal's body, all covered with maggots. I threw it across the room.

At our screams, Mom's boyfriend Jim came in with the biggest smile, laughing. *I was wondering how long it would take y'all to find that!*

∴

I could no longer protect my siblings; that much was clear.

There was the time Jim slammed Thovas's hand in a door and held it shut until all my brother's fingernails popped off. His hands shake to this day.

And then, one night, Jim tried to kill us all.

I'd taken a job bussing tables and washing dishes at a seafood restaurant across the golf course from where we lived. A few months prior, Anna had insisted I drive the old Chevy Impala she'd had for a minute to get her a Diet Coke from a specific corner store where they were the coldest. I was only fourteen, and I didn't know the gas from the brake from the clutch, and of course, I got in a wreck, totaled a neighbor's car, and sent Amy into the windshield. I'd had to take the job to pay back our neighbor for the damage and the stitches in my sister's face.

I worked nights because I was underage, and, anyway, that's the only spare time I had. As I got Amy and Thovas cleaned up and tucked in before my shift, I heard Jim in the kitchen rooting around in the silverware drawer. Anna was either passed out, watching TV, or just not helping in any capacity. As I walked to the door to leave, Jim appeared in the living room holding the biggest knife in the house. He pointed it right at me as my hand hovered over the knob. I looked at my brother and sister, and I knew I couldn't leave.

Jim directed all of us, Mom included, to sit in a circle on the floor and not move a muscle. We couldn't eat, speak, or go to the bathroom. Most especially, we weren't allowed to fall asleep. If it looked like one of us was nodding out, Jim held the knife blade to our necks, even Amy's. He said if we fell asleep, he'd kill us or gut our mother in front of us. Mom sat there, completely blank. I figured she was scared, or maybe she was in on it, but now I think she just entirely dissociated.

For twelve hours, we sat there like terrified monks, unable to even whimper. I'm sure we all peed ourselves; I don't really remember. Things became hazy as Jim ranted some insane monologue and Mom sunk deeper and deeper away. My adrenaline was all over the place, back and forth between leaden waves of absolute exhaustion and sudden shudders like I was falling from a treetop.

And just like that, Jim fell asleep. He passed out right in the middle of what he was saying—like someone had unplugged him. Even though my legs were tingly asleep, I jolted up and ran to the kitchen, where I grabbed an iron skillet from the stove. Before I could even think, I went back into the living room and conked Jim on the head HARD. I'd wanted to make good and sure he stayed out like a light for a long time so we could all escape, but—wouldn't you know it—the blow woke him right back up. He shot at me, raging and screaming, and I ran.

By myself, out the front door, down the stairs, and down the street. I got to an old friend's house, picked up the phone to call the cops, but panicked. *What if they take Thovas and Amy away?* Instead, I called my grandmother, Louise. As soon as the details of what had happened left my lips, I hung up the phone and fell asleep right there on the kitchen floor.

When I returned home the next day, Jim was gone. Mom didn't speak a word about the incident, but I got a beating for hitting him on the head and then bailing on everyone.

∴

In the months following the hostage incident, we moved again, a few times. I turned fifteen. And then we got Sadie.

Sadie was a retired police dog we'd happened to inherit from our friend, Fannie. Fannie knew my family from our Banana days. She was a little old lady who lived in a junker's paradise. Just piles of stuff in Franny's yard and all of it good. Somehow, this stooped German Shepherd had turned up among the open-air aisles of crazed pinball machines and wrought-iron bed frames, limping through the dry dandelions. When we visited Fannie this time, she looked at us all funny. I'm sure none of us seemed right at that point.

But Fannie knew better than to try to talk about it—instead, she insisted we take Sadie. Mom could be a complete monster, but she was pure sugar to people like Fannie, and it wasn't an act. In the outside world, her inner child still wanted to trust people who had good in them, and she showed them her best Anna. That's why she let us keep Sadie.

Sadie had been through so much and was suffering. Our thin-ass mattress was right on the floor, so even with her hips, she could step onto it and sleep with us kids at night. She was old and slept a lot, but she'd been a police dog and helped us feel a little safer. We needed that dog, and she needed us, and she was one of the best things that ever happened to me, Amy, and Thovas.

Mom didn't show any affection for Sadie or pay her much mind at all. And anyway, Anna had found a new man—a towering Polish guy named Joe, who rivaled Jim in his alcoholism and sadism. Jim and Joe were two sides of the same tired coin in Mom's jukebox bowl of quarters. It was the same old song.

One night, we kids were snuggling on the floor with Sadie when Anna and Joe flew in the door, loud and mean-laughing. In the kitchen, I heard Mom going on about something not up to par in there, some dirty fork or a smudge on a juice glass, and then she was all over me with a whole new kind of fury. Thovas and Amy skittered away and Sadie herded them against the wall.

This one lasted for what felt like hours. Some entity within Anna was regarding me differently now, as an older child. Plus, she had a cheering section. Joe whooped and hollered at Anna's rage and, at some point, he jumped on in. They took turns and ganged up, ripping my hair out in clumps and kicking me in the ribs and spine and skull. When one particular blow knocked the air outta me, I heard as from the end of a tunnel, the sound of Sadie growling.

None of us had ever heard Sadie growl before. It stopped Mom and Joe in their tracks. I was curled up on the floor, gasping for air, unable to scream as I watched Joe lunge at Sadie, grab her by the scruff, and throw her full-force across the room.

From where I lay, I saw Sadie hit the wall and heard one sharp yelp that I felt in my own lungs. As her body slid down parallel to mine, I could tell by the way she was laying with her tongue hanging out that she was gone. Joe yanked Sadie's body from my field of vision and flung her out the front door, which he slammed behind him. Then he picked me up like a baby and heaved me onto the floor in an adjacent room. It hurt to breathe; it hurt to blink. My brain hammered against my skull as I heard a metallic sound, then Mom's voice, maniacal.

I can't take this anymore. I'm gonna finish her off.

The familiar sharp slide of someone fishing through the knife drawer set off something in me similar to the day I was born. *Get out of here; she's really gonna do it this time.*

The window inside the room Joe had tossed me into had been painted shut for as long as we lived there. This time, I had no instrument to smash the pane—or strength to try. The way my head was turned, all I could see was Thovas sitting by that window, and I knew I had to survive for him.

Quiet as I could, I dragged myself to the window as Mom searched for the perfect weapon. I knew it was only a matter of time. I had to try at least. With each slap and drag of my palms, I prayed. To Mary and Jesus and every saint I'd ever seen or dreamed of, to my dad and my grandparents, to Sadie and Crystal and the gerbils and all my friends. I cashed in on every falling star wish and dandelion whisper. As I placed my shaking hands on the sill, I just surrendered and said,

Please, God, let it open.

∴

We believe that when we're talking to God we're talking to someone outside of ourselves. But really, we're appealing to the power within every one of us that can make miracles happen. Sometimes, it takes a moment of acute pressure for all that coal to focus itself into a diamond, cutting, and crystal clear.

The point of no return is the point along a journey where turning back would take longer than going forward, and falling would mean certain death. It's not a place but a moment. A surrender and a surge. This is the threshold of survival.

I looked Thovas straight in the eye and told him, *Please don't worry. No matter what, I will come back for you and Amy. I love you forever.*

The window opened.

I have no idea how I got my butt up and through that window. It was like those superhuman feats of strength where a mother would lift a whole car to save her babies. Only this time, I was saving myself. I was jumping from a burning building again, and I landed on my knees in every sense.

∴

There are two kinds of mending: visible and invisible.

Invisible mending tries to get the garment to look as close as possible to its original condition. Matched-up threads and exactly measured seams, like nothing happened at all. I understand not being able to buy new clothes and not wanting to draw attention to that. But it's the visible mending that heals.

I didn't have a choice in the matter. My clothes, myself, everything was a point of wear. It was all full of holes.

Visible mending is deliberate. But that doesn't mean it's contrived. Layers of story appear upon us with or without our choosing to display them. We're all walking around with these patches, these stories, this pain. Every single one of us. It's the running stitch that connects us, and it doesn't help a thing to hide it.

Patching something isn't ignoring it or even really fixing it. It's acknowledging that this thing happened to me. I am human. I am vulnerable. I fell, but I got back up.

Here now, lemme help you.

Chapter 8

DAYDREAMER
WORKWEAR

CRAWLING IS THE BASIS OF BALANCE—GETTING A PURCHASE
on gravity and momentum. It's an incredibly complex process our bodies
and brains build upon to understand walking and running.

That night, as soon as my knees hit the ground, I had to start from
square one. All I could focus on was the next circle of light thrown by the
streetlamps, illuminating the asphalt beneath my bleeding palms. A few
neighborhood dogs barked at the sorry sight of me, but otherwise, all was
quiet. If anyone spotted me, they sure as shit kept it to themselves.

On all fours, dragging my scraped knees behind me, I headed toward
the only place I knew could soothe. I have no idea how long it took for
me to crawl those seven blocks, but I finally made it to my father's house.

∴

My knuckles wouldn't form a fist; I slapped Preston's front door with
my flat hand. When he opened it, alarmed not to find me at eye level, he
immediately crouched down and burst into tears. He gathered me up

into his arms and laid me in the back seat of his car, drove to pick up my Grandmother Brown, and then went to University Hospital.

I had multiple broken ribs. Scrapes and bruises screamed across my scrawny frame. Huge patches of my hair had been ripped out. Both of my eyes were completely swollen shut. I could feel my body being bandaged and stitched and poked and set, and I heard as they gave the order to call the authorities. I tried to lie about what had happened, even then: I'd fallen, been beaten up by neighborhood kids—old habits for a diehard.

But what had been done to me broke the spirit of every law. My father at my side whispered, *Kid, this time you have to tell them.* So I did.

I don't know what became of the police report—if anyone went out to check on my siblings or sent someone after Mom or Joe. As soon as I left the hospital, I moved in with my dad. I didn't see Mom, or Thovas, or Amy for a year.

∴

Healing, for me, always meant time with Dad.

In the few months after I crawled to his door, I recuperated under my father's watch. He changed my bandages and fed me, guided meditations for us both. He handed me tools: pencils and paints, a guitar. His girlfriend taught me two songs, "Needle and the Damage Done" by Neil Young, and "Here Comes the Sun" by George Harrison. I plunked through the chords as Dad sat at the foot of my bed. Scabby knuckles cracked and then softened; my tired heart found a place to rest.

I got a friend to sneak into Anna's house to snag my skateboard and a Supertramp record—my prized possessions, all I owned in the world after the guitar. I did have one pair of old Vans, but otherwise, I wore my father's denim work shirts and white V-necks, his 501s with the extra-long Levite hems rolled up around my ankles. Once I was well enough, I'd put the Supertramp record under my arm and push off to my friends' houses, where we'd listen to it over and over.

As much as I missed Amy and Thovas each moment and worried over them endlessly, I was finding an inner equilibrium. That was always my quest, in a way. From the back of a motorcycle to the top of a tree, to a bicycle with two kids hanging on me, to a skateboard—with each successive outlook, I challenged myself to find balance.

Crawling had recalibrated my self-reliance; I began to see things I wanted and imagine how I could attain them. I wanted to go to school; I wanted to make art and create a place in the world for myself, from where I could provide for my siblings. I focused on this like the horizon cresting each hill on my skateboard.

⁘

As smart as my father was—as much as he could lose himself in philosophy, research, and poetry—he didn't know how to locate the language of disappointment. Only something big and physical could exorcize this emotion. Large-scale paintings and murals fit the bill. Swatting at blank planes with brushes and colors, creating. Other times, he just exploded and reacted. Destroyed.

I idealized my father, who idealized the world. When life didn't match up with the picture he painted in his mind, he slashed the canvas. Shattered jars of rocks on the roadside. Dragged my brother and me to the morgue. More.

As much as I was Preston's protégé, I was also a teenager. I was free from my mom's abuse for the first time in my life. I wanted to skate until my face hurt from smiling. Laugh until I collapsed. Listen to every kind of music and howl at the moon with kids my age.

One night, I was out a little later than Preston had liked. Maybe he was using again or kicking again—itching in his burnt skin that still stung. He was smoking-mad on the porch, ready to pounce. No sooner had I rolled up to him he grabbed my board right from under me. Hollering and banging it against the pavement, over and over. When it didn't give, he ransacked the house looking for something that would.

With a guttural *TWANG*, he grabbed my guitar by the neck and smashed it Kurt Cobain-style on the ground until it was all strings and splinters and hollowness.

Every breath Preston had stirred from my soles was sucked out. It was a punch in the gut.

This was so fucking uncool. And I knew I didn't deserve it. I grabbed my unbreakable board and scooted off with the clothes on my back.

∴

Maybe you don't have shit besides a skateboard and a Supertramp record, but if you have one true friend, you have everything. For me, that friend was Jennifer Doyle.

Jennifer and I'd met back in the Banana Funk N' Junk days. From the moment we laid eyes on each other, we were in lockstep shenanigans, always and forever banished together. Each wound—and there were so many between us—was bathed with tears that rolled down our cheeks as much from laughter as from pain. Hand-in-hand, we ran headlong across minefields.

That night, I skated straight to Jennifer's door. They welcomed me in, but they didn't allow me to stay. Jennifer's family had their own shit, as they all do. And yeah, Jennifer and I had gotten into some trouble together.

There was the time we'd been arrested skinny dipping with friends in the public pool. And the time we decided to hitchhike across San Antonio. We'd gotten right into the first truck that pulled over, and the second we did, we knew something wasn't right. The driver locked the doors and pulled off in the opposite direction. There were no handles on the interior passenger doors. I wrapped my arms around Jennifer in one second and yelled, *HOLD ON TIGHT!* I aimed my foot at the door panel and kicked that thing as hard as I could. Only the grace of God allowed it to fly open.

Jennifer and I launched ourselves from the truck. Mercifully, we missed the pavement and landed on the shoulder, where we rolled and rolled and rolled, coming to a stop in a patch of grass. The driver sped off, and all was quiet and eerily still. I was 100 percent sure we were dead. But somehow, we were fine. A little banged up, but okay. Jennifer and I looked at each other and burst into laughter mixed with tears. Then we got up and held hands and ran like hell.

I hid behind Jennifer's tall frame the night of the smashed guitar as she flat-out denied to her dad that I was even in the house. I was small and easy to conceal among the hoarder-style stacks of magazines and mail that towered through each inch of her home. A pushed-together pile of blankets between the couch and the wall became my nest, where I slept on and off for a few months.

∴

Not every creature gets fresh hay and wildflower stems to build a nest. You use what you have, and your home must be built anew, over and over. I stowed away at Jennifer's as much as I could and slept at other friends' houses here and again, but many nights that year saw me without a sure place to stay.

My parents had obliterated every shred of security in my life, but somehow, I still had faith in the support of the world, the universe, and nature. Anna and Preston's examples had been shitty, but their lessons were sound: there is always beauty and joy to be found, especially on the ground.

Right before my father got burned, he and I used to visit this one junkyard. It was a random dump across the developing McAllister freeway where people chunked all their old furniture and home goods. We'd walk through the construction to that dump every day, and if there was an old couch or television, we'd put together a whole living room—shove a jacked-up La-Z-Boy into the scene, prop up a makeshift coffee table. Grab an old soup can and put flowers in it. Dad might find an old nail and, using a rock, hammer it into one of the scrubby mesquites nearby. Hang up a busted painting or an old empty wooden picture frame. We made these little weird houses with no walls and no ceilings, and then we'd sit there together watching sunset TV.

Each day, we'd return to find everything was different. People had plucked their junk back, inspired by our arrangements. So we'd just create a whole new view.

I kept the vision of these outdoor living rooms in my heart those houseless nights. I'd ride my skateboard until I was flat-out exhausted, crumpling on someone's front lawn to look up at the stars and the moon. Then I'd hop back on the board and roll to one of my revolving spots of sanctuary: the grounds of the McNay Art Institute, beneath the trees in Brackenridge Park, along the banks of the San Antonio River, among the historical missions. From where I lay, I dreamed of a home down to the tiniest detail: what the silverware would look like and where it would go, what plants I would grow, what colors and rugs and art. What the bed would feel like and the warm bath.

I was exposed and vulnerable, but still, I felt sheltered. Laying on the grass, it was like luminous fibers from the Earth herself tangled with the vine-like tendrils of my crazy hair. I felt held and safe, safer than I had in a long time. I took these filaments of faith in hand and wove my own little nest within.

∴

The coolest thing about making a safe space for your inner child is that it attracts other gentle souls. In the most innocent and affirming way, they want to come play. It's like your imaginary friends become embodied, joining you in the real-life quests you'd once dreamed up.

Jennifer's mom, Neva, was a fashion illustrator for the *San Antonio Express-News*. Even though I hid from her husband to sleep at their home, Neva welcomed me at her kitchen table openly, giving me lessons on sketching fashion. It was the very first time I ever talked about clothing design with someone who gave a shit and wasn't out to punish me for these dreams; the first time I felt free to envision that fashion could become a career.

And even though she was unaware of it, Neva nurtured my deepest desire at the time: to go to high school. I couldn't provide security for my siblings then, but I wanted to in the future. No one in my immediate family had a diploma, and I wanted to be the first. I used Jennifer's address to enroll myself in Alamo Heights High School. A forgery of my mom's flowery signature, and that was that. The spirit of the law saw that this one particular dream had a chance of becoming real.

By Anna

I stayed quiet as a mouse in the mornings until Jennifer's dad left for work. I often didn't get a chance to shower, so I'd brush my teeth and wash my face in the water hose outside, and skate straight to school. I went every single day.

Art and track were my favorite subjects. My art teacher, Ms. Aickles, was a kind and gentle woman who sometimes invited me over for dinner. She'd play loud opera music and cook vegetarian food, tell me about the lives of my favorite artists, and place in my lap stacks of coffee-table books she'd gathered from used bookstores.

My track coach was just as kind, at least at first. I was like fuckin' Forrest Gump, man; I could get in that zone and *go*. Coach recognized my commitment and passion; she bought me proper running shoes, sweatsuits, and jackets. She even invited me into her home for hearty dinners after meets. I felt so happy and blessed to have angels like her in my life, people I could trust who were teaching me lifesaving shit. I sat on her couch one evening and told her this very thing when suddenly her hands were all over me—groping my chest and rubbing my thighs.

With every shred of strength from my toes to my fingertips, fueled by pure anger and disbelief, I pushed her off of me. I screamed at her, loud, and ran the fuck out. Straight back to Jennifer's house.

∴

I didn't know who to trust anymore, but I trusted Jennifer.

That evening, Neva asked us to rake all the leaves in the front yard into a big pile. She brought stacks of clean sheets and linens to place on top, making a giant leaf pallet. Jennifer and I laid on this bed of leaves for hours that night, staring at the stars and telling each other where we wanted to be in twenty-five years. We talked about love and magic and how, no matter what, we'd always be together. We climbed an oak in Jennifer's yard and hung upside-down, laughing when our T-shirts slid around our necks cuz we didn't have any boobs.

Our bodies had been betrayed, but our hearts still beat.

The next day at school, my track coach cornered me. She shamed me for accepting food and shoes. I emptied my locker and quit the team. I knew I hadn't done anything to warrant the abuse. I was tired of the narrative that it was all my fault. I had proven to myself I could rise from my knees. I was ready to stop running.

∵

And then there was Kelly.

I'd known Kelly since fifth grade. He'd always been kind and non-judgmental, a beautiful kid with long eyelashes and blond hair parted neatly to the side. Our souls clasped onto each other in the sweetest way, and we were the best of friends from the very beginning. He'd climb a tree with me or watch the stars, sit me on the handlebars of his bike, and ride all over the city. The children within me and Kelly knew each other from the instant I saw his hazel eyes. By the time I was fifteen, we were head-over-heels in love.

More than anyone I'd ever met, Kelly supported me, advocated for me, and cared for me. His life was *Leave It to Beaver* compared to mine, and while I didn't move in with him, I was permitted to sleep over in his little sister's room here and there.

I'd never felt that way about anyone until that point. When it felt right, I lost my virginity to him that year, which was huge for me. I felt safe. With Kelly, I never lost myself. As much as I loved him and as much as our lives became intertwined, Kelly always respected my autonomy and promoted my sense of adventure.

Plus, he had a truck.

∵

So many weekends, Kelly and I, along with Jennifer and other ragtag kids, would pool together whatever money we could find to see music: AC/DC and Fleetwood Mac at the coliseum in San Antonio, Iggy Pop, Blondie, the Sex Pistols, and the Ramones at the Armadillo World Headquarters in Austin. We'd go to the rodeo and see George Strait, have makeshift picnics at free symphony concerts in the park, and sneak into punk clubs to watch Wendy O. Williams with her duct-taped nipples and whipped cream and chainsaws.

Each concert had a whole different vibe. I lost myself in observing what people wore and how they moved. I absorbed all the accessories, from lip rings or tattoos to kicker cowboy boots scuffed from farm work. It was a dazzling, loud circus of influences and textures. I didn't have Mom or Dad in my ear challenging my self-expression and my right to wear what I wanted. So I tried it all on.

Besides the shows, I spent whatever cash I'd earned—cleaning people's garages and fish tanks and birdcages—at the thrift store. From infancy, I'd crawled around on the dirty floors beneath thrift-store racks, reaching up to those cast-off cottons and dust-bunny velvets like they were mobiles over my crib. It was as much my home as anything. Ten bucks was a fortune; with it, I could assemble an entire wardrobe. Men's thrashed 501 jeans and Converse tennis shoes. Loose-fitting metal band T-shirts and vintage dresses with moth-eaten holes in them. Combat boots and flannel shirts. Hand-crocheted bikinis, suede platforms, and chunky, bamboo flip-flops with toe socks. Black fishnets and black lipstick and black fingernail polish.

For the first time, I could be a kid. I wasn't gonna screw that up by trying to have fun the way a lot of teenagers do, with alcohol and drugs. Teenagers want to pretend they're adults, but most of the adults I knew were fucked up and shuttered down. I didn't wanna inhabit that world; that shit was entirely too familiar, and anyway, those substances just made me sick to my soul.

∴

Preston had always said that for as beautiful and open a thing could be, the opposite is also true. He'd led me through that metaphysical terrain in literal paths of Fire and Ice. We could both be so starry-eyed and so damn stubborn. I wasn't ready to return to him. Nope, not until he apologized.

I learned that a few months after I'd escaped Anna's last attempt to end my life, she'd had another nervous breakdown and checked herself into rehab. Thovas now lived with Preston, and Amy lived with a friend in Austin. I'd quit running, but Mom had reported me to the authorities as a runaway. I certainly had momentum then, but she had it all wrong—for the first time in my life, I was running toward something instead of away.

∴

They say home is where the heart is, but I think it's more accurate to say that your heart is your home—riding around inside of your body, in cahoots with your brilliant brain that weaves all your senses together, guiding your form to carve creative shapes in the midst of what looks like falling.

Skateboarding isn't merely point A to point B, but a point of evolution and invention—embodied architecture. Play.

I make clothes for this play, this movement. Maybe it's baggy jeans you can skate in, patched up for protection and embellished with icons of freedom. Or perhaps play looks like spinning in a twirly dress punctuated with eyelets and tattered lace. It could be hand to your heart in a cotton nightgown, in gratitude to exist at all. We were put here to play, to delight and invent, and move.

Many of the spots I spent hours skateboarding, along with a group of young old souls we collectively referred to as the J-Boys, were beneath the same overpasses where Preston and I had thrown up those ephemeral red stone murals. My father had shown me how to make everyday use of the seemingly useless; skating showed me this applied to landscape, to cityscape. A wonderland created from abandoned spaces by those who had been similarly discarded.

This sense of play permeated the murals my father did, the outdoor living rooms. And for all her fucked-upness, it also shimmied through Anna's creations. But that time in my life was a time to move through the world on my terms, with my eyes and palms focused on the next spot of light ahead of my board, a constellation of sidewalk oracles linked to a bright horizon.

Chapter 9

EMBROIDERY

IN EMBROIDERY, THERE'S AS MUCH UNDOING AS THERE IS doing—plucking and pulling your thread back through the holes you pierced to see where you might have gone off-course and where you might begin again. Our ancestors once believed the stars themselves resulted from this kind of occurrence: pinpricks of light poked into the fabric of night. The Creator doesn't make mistakes, but sometimes it's so damn hard to see the reason.

From what I can figure, the branch of mathematics called Chaos Theory tells us that the endless entanglement of existence, as random as it may seem, actually follows a kind of order—a pattern. You might not be able to understand it or predict it, but you can trust it. It's beautiful and scary, and maybe the only thing that's certain.

As I sat in class at the end of tenth grade in 1978, not thinking about any of this stuff, the most gifted instructor of Chaos Theory casually reentered my life. A little slip of paper with my name on it beckoned me to the school office. The moment I opened the door, the scent of jungle gardenia hit me like a wall. There she stood in a beautiful hand-embroidered Romanian blouse that was sheer as shit and hid nothing. Silver bangles stacked up her forearms, and flowers in all phases of decay stuck into her hair.

Mom.

Let's go, she said. *I've already unenrolled you from here, anyway.*

⁘

Signatures from Anna's actual hand were never etched with the intention of doing, only undoing.

There were to be no goodbyes with my friends or finishing tenth grade. No embracing or tears or explanations. I grabbed my skateboard from my locker and followed Mom's jangly click-clack out to the parking lot as a battered space rock sucked back into orbit.

Anna leaned against the flagpole, smoking a cigarette. She told me she'd moved to Austin, and she needed my help. It wasn't a question. I got into the car with just the clothes on my back. As she sped up I-35, the wind swirling from rolled-down windows blended with the radio cranked up loud, lulling me into a deep sleep. A while later, sudden silence and stillness jolted me awake. The Pinto had come to rest in a vast parking lot of an apartment complex.

It was like another world, sudden and strange. As my senses returned, I remembered Amy. My little sister was there somewhere.

Mom knew right where, and I followed her to the door. As soon as it opened, Amy bounced straight into my arms. She squeezed my neck so tight. Her weight against my chest brought me back to Earth. She was four-and-a-half now, still a skinny thing but stronger, healthy, and near to flourishing.

My little sister had been living in Austin for a few months with a woman named Maggie. Once Mom's AA sponsor, Maggie was solid and sweet and adored my little sister. She managed the apartment complex we were standing in and secured Anna a job there and a unit next door. I'd live with Mom, and Amy would stay with Maggie, but together, we'd all start anew—a village in neighboring little boxes.

My brain began rearranging the details of this new reality like living-room furniture. The apartment complex was bare but clean, built into the hills of the Travis Heights neighborhood in Austin, just south of Town

Lake. Once I could work up enough scratch to get a new board, there were sloping streets to skateboard on. We were right across from Travis High School, which I enrolled myself in with yet another forgery. I'd look after Amy and help around the apartments to earn a little money. My friends could visit.

It seemed doable. Possible. Bearable.

∴

With Amy on my lap, her forehead to mine, all I could feel was gratitude. But I couldn't remain in that space. There was too much to do, and it wasn't Amy's responsibility to keep me centered. It *was,* apparently, my responsibility to hold that space for my mother.

Anna could no more sit still with her children than she could with the anxieties and fears that racked her brain. Quiet moments screamed at her; inaction was unbearable, but the next right thing was too strict a path. She *had* to spiral. As the world's greatest victim, she felt she deserved to burn.

I was there to keep Amy fed, the dishes washed, the laundry put away. To be a somewhat steady element, like gravity, that follows a pattern and provides a sliver of predictability.

Chaos Theory tries to show us that the only thing we can surely expect is the unexpected. But chaos *was* Anna's pattern. I never knew what to expect or not expect. Everything was, and is, constantly changing. All I could do at that still point was polish the mismatched thrift-store silverware and keep dancing.

∴

She tried for a moment. Mom showed up at jobs and stuck around me and Amy for a while. But within a month, Anna started pocketing all the security deposits and tenants' monthly rent. I was doing her work, not getting paid, and taking care of my sister. I got kicked out of school for not having proper immunizations. There was Tecate in the fridge and pills everywhere. Mom was using again and dating scumbags.

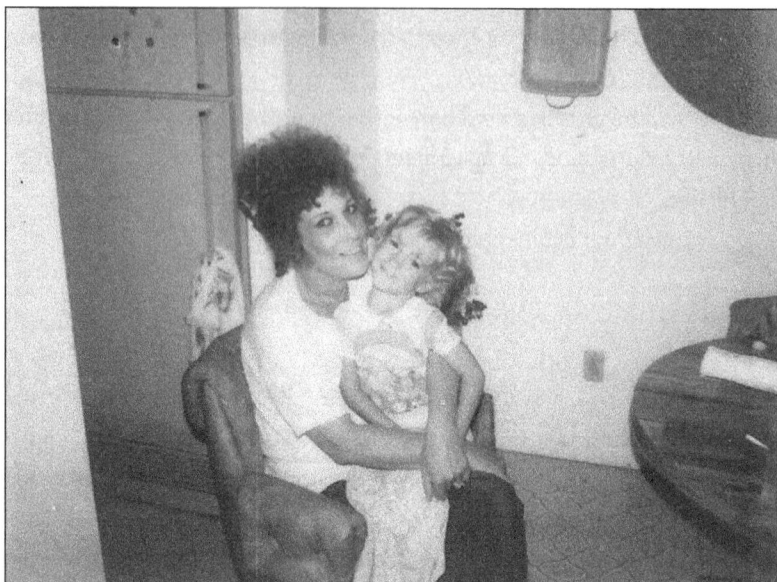

Anna and Amy

It was the same nightmare, and I wanted to wake myself up from within it.

One afternoon, when I hadn't cleaned the apartment to her liking, Mom snapped into attack mode. I'd slipped into emotional sleepwalking, but her balled-up fist aimed at my head woke me up. Something inside me reached out and caught her arm mid-strike.

Enough, I told her.

She looked at me like she'd seen a ghost. I had never done that before. I was older now and stronger than her. And she knew it. She never laid a hand on me again.

⁂

But Anna was vengeful and capable. The few belongings I'd collected in those mere months in Austin—some raggedy T-shirts and worn jeans, painted canvases, and used records—became the epicenter of Mom's frustration. Unable to strike me, instead, she flung open the sliding door and threw every last item of mine over the balcony into the pool. I quietly walked to the office and called Kelly collect on the pay phone. Twiddling the silver rat-tail cord and checking for change in the coin return, I watched as everything I owned—the talismans of my struggle to settle—soared from Anna's hands. As soon as I knew Kelly was on his way, I clicked the phone into its cradle, grabbed the pool skimmer, and tried to save what I could.

Over the roar of Anna's insults, I walked to Maggie's apartment and pulled Amy's string bean arms and legs into my lap. Buried my nose into her hair, inhaling that little spot on her head that still smelled like a baby. I kissed and kissed her, rocking her back and forth until Kelly arrived sometime later. Again, I looked my little sister in the eyes and told her I loved her. That I'd be back to get her real soon. That, I promised, again.

And again.

∴

Back up I-35 with Kelly, staring out the window at the straight-shot terrain, I felt exhausted all over. We reached his family home, where I was allowed to stay and welcomed in with open arms. It was a peaceful place full of kids and plants and love. The most enormous magnolia tree in the whole neighborhood stood in their front yard, so grand they named the street after it. At the end of the block, a wide green space filled with old solid oaks opened upon the banks of the flowing San Antonio River.

Kelly's mom, Marcine, was a teacher, and she encouraged me to go right back to school. But the routine of enrolling and unenrolling, doing and undoing had all become too much. Out of the question. I just wanted to get a job, my own place. A new life for me, Thovas, and Amy.

On the days Kelly went to school, I wandered around his neighborhood, rustling up a little work and saving every penny I earned. When he returned in the afternoons, we'd walk to the river and climb up in the oaks, staying out so late Marcine had to pad down there in her nightgown at sundown to fetch us. Sometimes, we followed her back, and sometimes, we stayed snuggled up there 'til sunrise. Kelly would go back to school in the morning, and I would lay my head down in his little sister's frilly pink room to rest among the Kewpie dolls and Cabbage Patch Kids.

I often found myself in my old neighborhood, strolling for hours along the sidewalks where my siblings and I had lugged our few belongings. I even found work cleaning the same houses we'd lived in. It was a crazy dot-to-dot trail that curled and crossed itself like a ballroom dance diagram. I followed its steps until they led me to the last place we'd all lived together, where I had escaped through the window.

The house itself sat like a scene within a snow globe—I'd never been able to see it clearly for all the shit snarling around. I hadn't realized how beautiful it all was. My family had only occupied the bottom floor of the home's towering three-story Victorian majesty. I didn't remember ever noticing the little garage off to one side—the one that just so happened to have a cute little apartment right on top—and a sign in the window that read, "For Rent, $100 a month."

I'd saved up just that much. I had found my place.

∴

Kelly and I had started up a real jack-of-all-trades business cleaning houses and maintaining yards, painting fences, and fixing what needed to be fixed for people we'd seen since childhood. On days when the labor was especially tough and the temperatures especially high, which was always, all I could think about was the Ice of jumping in the river.

You are truly blessed if you're lucky enough to grow up near a river. There's a sacred spot on the San Antonio where my dad taught us to swim. One afternoon I rode my bike down to the exact place, plopped my tired butt down on the concrete of the low-water crossing where Thovas and I used to dive right in with our father. My legs dangled from frayed 501 cut-offs, and I leaned back on my hands to watch the sunlight's disco-ball glint on the surface.

Fuck, man. I missed my dad.

My feet blurred beneath the current as my tears slinked into the stream. There were many people around that day, shouting and splashing and carrying on. But over all the commotion, this one sound found me loud and clear; the tick of a ten-speed bike being walked along clicked in my ears like sonar. It sounded like my dad's old bike, but I figured that was crazy. Don't all bikes sound the same?

I didn't look up when the ticking stopped cold at my side; I refused to believe it could be true until Preston's feet appeared in the river right next to mine, and his scent of coffee, cigarettes, and paint, familiar to me as anything, overcame my senses.

For maybe half a second, when our eyes met, it was over a vast void, a chasm of time and hurt with a smashed guitar at the bottom. But it filled back up with love just like that. We didn't need to talk about the why or the where. Everything fell away. It was all water. We were the bridge.

I sobbed and hugged him. *Let's never do that again, OK?* He submitted. *I promise*, I replied, even though it hadn't been my fault.

I wasn't about to hash it all out. It was a miracle. Yet again, the sound of Preston's two wheels has heralded his return.

∴

A few days later, I reunited with Thovas. He was ten years old now, a little metalhead skateboard punk like me. In some ways, it felt like a hundred years had passed since we'd locked eyes the night Anna tried to kill me. In other ways, it was more like one second. We just held on to each other and cried and cried.

Dad gave Thovas a lot more freedom than he had afforded me; their relationship was more easy-breezy. Mom had always been the same with Thovas, even more lax than Dad, and that summer of 1980, my brother got the bright idea to go stay with her in Austin. I tried to talk him out of it but had to let him go. All he really wanted to do was skateboard and go to record stores. I had to trust he could get by on all we'd learned together.

Just a few weeks into his trip, I received a collect call from the same damn pay phone by the pool that I'd used only months earlier. I couldn't understand what he was saying, but he needed us immediately. Kelly and I jumped in the truck and sped to Austin right back up I-35. We arrived to find Anna lying on the floor of their apartment in a puddle of vomit and what appeared to be blood. It was the first time I had seen her since leaving Austin the day she threw all my belongings into the pool.

She's dead, she's dead, Thovas cried.

One of Mom's boyfriends had beaten her up, slashed up furniture and canvases with a knife, and then threatened to kill Thovas. My brother was in shock. I held his shaking hands as a neighbor called 911. The very second EMS found signs of life in my mother and loaded her into the ambulance, I piled Thovas and his skateboard into Kelly's truck and headed in the opposite direction—right back down the interstate's clogged artery.

The home we returned to was no longer the cute little garage apartment. Somewhere along the way of our work, Kelly and I had wandered past a new place: Trail Street was a little gravel alleyway that ended in a cul-de-sac, almost totally hidden in the middle of our neighborhood. Another old Victorian that had been vacant for many years stood in disrepair at the end, completely falling apart and beautiful. The rent was the same as our little garage apartment. So we took it.

We'd just begun renovations, balancing chaos with order. We loved how the home was deteriorating and only set out to fix what was needed to make it livable. This was where we brought Thovas home for a few days, and it was where, a few months later, Anna appeared on our doorstep.

∴

It doesn't matter where you live; chaos returns under different guises, different masks, to other addresses. This was Anna in classic banshee form, completely and utterly hell-bent on destruction—smeared eye makeup and a heavy slur, swaying and reeking to the heavens. She'd borrowed someone's van, which she'd driven up onto our lawn, parked cattywampus and still running. Amy's panicked cries from inside the van found my ears.

All fluid rage, Anna focused one bleary eye on me and told me she'd come to say goodbye. She was fixin' to kill herself and Amy by driving them both off a cliff. My fight response was no match for Anna's flight. Even in her condition, she sprinted straight to the van, threw that clunker into drive, and tried to run me over right there on the lawn. I froze as I watched Amy's terrified face, her hand pushing flat against the glass. I hollered for Kelly, and we followed them in our truck. But they were gone.

Another instance of retracing steps. We drove past every old haunt and jaunt of Mom's, every old friend's address. Nothing. The last place I could think of was the last place I heard she may have lived in San Antonio, another random roach motel. We found the van, parked right up on the front yard in the same sideways angle, again still running. The front door of the house was flung wide open; we entered to find Anna passed out on the living room floor.

I followed the faint sound of Amy's whimpers to a room where she was hiding under a bed. I scooped her up just as gently and quietly as I could, and we tiptoed past Anna's prone body. Clinging to me, Amy whispered she wanted her backpack from the van. As I reached in to switch off the ignition and grab the bag, I saw the entire front seat and floorboard was just solid with syringes, covered in blood spatters, the whole nine yards.

It's Mommy's medicine, was all Amy said. I got the little backpack, slammed the door, and buckled us in together in Kelly's truck. As we drove away, Amy's tiny trembles began to stabilize. With each block, her breath evened out. Her face nuzzled into my neck, butterfly kisses from her long eyelashes slowing their urgent fluttering into small sighs.

I know you love Momma, but you're never going to be with her again, I told my baby sister, rubbing her back in circles and kissing the side of her head. She sniffed and nodded and pulled herself a centimeter closer to me before she loosened, slack into the instant deep sleep of the spellbound.

⁘

For several months, Amy lived with us. Kelly and I worked our asses off to give her a good life. She danced around our tall ladders, blowing dandelions and racing dragonflies as we painted the house. We'd fill up the old claw-foot bathtub on the weed-choked front lawn with water from the hose, throw in some zinnias and wild rose petals, and plunk Amy right in there. She was always covered in mud or leaves or paint or scratchy weeds that clung like Velcro to her hand-me-downs.

But as lush and full of sun as our lives together could be, money was tight. Sometimes, our cupboards were plain bare. Amy and I'd been brought up on breadcrumbs, but I wanted her to thrive. One day, I found she'd eaten a whole bottle of Flintstones vitamins because she was so hungry. She deserved more.

I'd bought those months with Amy by paying off Anna. Whenever Mom came around to get Amy back, I just gave her money. It seemed to suffice, and Anna slunk away. But none of this was enough. I told my mother we had to give this child a fair chance; Amy needed to go back with Maggie. Maybe I caught Mom in a weak or semi-sober moment, but it didn't take much convincing. Plus, I offered her what little cash I had.

That very day, Anna signed over her rights to Amy. Maggie officially adopted my little sister soon after, and Amy moved back to Austin. I missed her every moment, and we piled miles on Kelly's truck, driving up and down old I-35.

⁂

Within turmoil, people are distracted and focused on their role in the roiling. Plus, chaos has momentum. The order within follows a rhythm. If you can ride that wave, you might be able to see a path. With everything blowing around, I did something just for me. And I did it without telling a soul.

One day, I biked down to a testing center and signed up to take the GED. I hadn't wanted anyone to know because I thought it'd jinx the whole thing. But I did it—by the skin of my teeth, but I fucking did it.

Kelly's mom, Marcine, was the first person I told. A few days later, she threw me a surprise graduation party with a cap and gown and cake and everything. No one from my family came: Mom was God-knows-where, Thovas didn't really care, and Preston always said that if you want to be educated all you need to do is get a library card. Between that and doing something creative every day, your mind would gather everything it needed. Diplomas or certificates were just "products," landmarks of the end of learning.

I'd just wanted to finish high school, man. That's it.

By that point, I'd picked up on the fact that life is just gonna keep teaching us shit, regardless. You might as well stay curious about the process—learning and unlearning all you can, stitch by undone stitch.

∴

Embroidery is beautiful not only for what you see, but for all you don't. It's a messy map from the back—absolute chaos, all switchbacks and starts. Knots upon knots, pulled with teeth and pricked fingers. Each one a prayer on a string.

Clothing creation is based on repetition. Over and over, up and under—the most intricate and beautiful flourishes, especially so. Hand embroidery is hunched over, fingers-flexed work, focusing on the next stitch like the lines of a highway, pulled by spirit to lay down something lovely amid all the old patterns that keep sucking you back in.

Two steps forward and one step back is still progress, binding us to stronger stuff. People can tell you all day long that you're strong. What's more helpful to hear is: Use your strength.

That's the step forward, stabilized.

Let your love be contagious
the light house across murky waters.
Show it even when
they don't deserve it

Because even if they
are too weary to accept it,
I promise they will still never forget it

Chapter 10

SAINTS

ANNA WAS SO FREE, BUT FOR ALL THE WRONG REASONS. SOME-times, though, she'd land. We might bump into her then, but we couldn't hold her. She was like sand. Like a cactus.

I'd long since stopped expecting love from my mother. But I never stopped wanting love *for* her—health and peace and mercy. Shakespeare wrote that mercy is not some grand gesture. It's natural and gentle, as rain falling from heaven.

My mother clung to every drop.

⁘

When rain shows up, it shows up. And when it doesn't, there's not a single thing you can do about it. After signing over her rights to my little sister, Anna appeared as the rain: there were periods of drought and flood, drama, and dullness. And then along came David.

David cropped up the same way Mom's other boyfriends and husbands had: suddenly, there was a gold band on Mom's finger and a new man in her house. The bar wasn't set real high, but David was actually lovely—small and neat, mild-mannered and sweet. He looked like a professor, all clean-cut in button-down shirts, with blond hair clipped close to his skull. He was all *yes ma'am* and *please* and *thank you*. Nothing was funky about him except his intellect, which was tremendous, and the fact that he was a mere twenty-five years old to Anna's forty-four.

We had no fucking clue what he was doing with our Mom, but from the start, it was clear David intended to be part of our family. He was like a lost little cat who wanted someone to open the door and let him in. The age difference between him and Anna dissolved as we all warmed to David's gentle influence. Our family was fucked up in so many ways, but one thing we weren't ever was judgmental. Anyone could sit at our table as long as they didn't mind a few plates flying around here and there.

∴

We never sat together as a family as much as when Anna was married to David. Some assortment of us would find ourselves at Mom and David's little apartment on the corner of San Pedro and Mulberry, right across the street from my old junior high. Sometimes, even Preston would come; he and David loved talking about God.

The smell of cumin tickled your nose whenever Anna cooked. Her favorite spice—dank and prickly just like her—danced with her jungle gardenia and made your head spin. For a *gringa*, Mom made the best Spanish rice with cheesy enchiladas and homemade salsas, clanging, slamming, and smoking as she cooked. David set the table impeccably, whistling along to Hank Williams on the stereo. Man, that guy could whistle. All trills and flourishes as he laid out the flatware just so.

Before we ate, David said some humble words to Jesus every single time. Thovas and I would bow our heads but glance at each other wide-eyed—that had certainly never happened before. I thought it was sweet.

After dinner, David did the damn dishes. I was spared that loaded chore. If that ain't mercy, then I don't know what is.

∴

As straight-arrow as he was, sometimes David disappeared. He'd borrow Mom's Ford Pinto and be gone for a few days. Anna would miss him and cry, and then he'd return. No one asked and he didn't explain, but he was gone too long once, and Mom was sure he'd left her. She frantically called hospitals, she drank, fell into a mess, dissolved. When a police officer showed up at her door a week or so later, she feared the worst.

But it was even worse than that.

Her car had been found in San Antonio with a dead body shoved into the back. David was in jail.

The internet didn't exist in 1981. There was no way for any of us to find out what might be going on. It wasn't on the news, and Mom didn't wanna know. If I'm really honest, I can say that none of us wanted to know. Our very survival had depended on secrecy and silence for so long, it felt unnatural to dig any deeper.

Piles of letters stamped by the state prison started to arrive almost immediately, soft-spoken appeals in a small script. Sweet and pleading, compelling. David insisted he was innocent; they had gotten the wrong guy, thrown off by a common name. I wanted to trust David so badly; the way that man had brought such peace to my family, whistling like that? He was a saint; no way he could be a murderer.

David's letters might've remained the end of our learning had it not been for Dad, for whom sheets of paper were only a means and never an end. Preston could withstand silence but never outright lies.

From the moment he was caught, David whistled a different tune to the cops. When all was said and done, he'd confessed to killing at least seven men over seven years. He began his spree in San Antonio in 1974 when he was nineteen years old, just one year older than I was right then, as I listened to my father read the report from the newspaper. I got chills. It got worse.

His victims ranged in age from eighteen to seventy-two. The tools and methods David used to end their lives were just ghastly: claw hammers and concrete blocks, ice picks, wooden posts, and knives—each instance, overkill.

Amid all that mayhem, David was arrested for burglary and spent a little time in jail, under the radar for his other crimes. I guess when he got out, he took a break from murdering, and this is when he'd met and married my mother.

∴

On paper, Anna should've been serial-killing right alongside her husband. All the markers were there: sensation-seeking, a lack of remorse, impulsivity, and a history of abuse. She could shut off ice-cold quick as a whip, just as she did when I told her of David's crimes. She was mainly pissed about losing her car.

I'd lived with violence for nineteen years. Though we didn't discuss it, we knew it was there. The volcano was part of the landscape. David's devil was different. He wasn't hotheaded but carefully calculating, even with the letters he sent. As he confessed to the cops, he was writing to us about his innocence and his love for our family. I wanted to believe that you can hold two different things in your mind and heart and have both of them be true at the same time. But hope can be a claw hammer.

I still get nauseous when I think about how intimate my family was with a real, true monster. How my brother and I sat in dark movie theaters with him, sharing buttered popcorn. What I grieved the most was how I believed my mother had found love again from someone kind. I guess mercy really is as indiscriminate as the rain—the reprieve we'd all felt from Anna's stability and joy had been ushered in by a man who withheld those same qualities toward his victims.

David's letters were only ever addressed to me or Preston and were only sent to Dad's house. They hardly ever mentioned Mom. At first, I thought maybe David couldn't face how much this was hurting her. But then it occurred to me that perhaps he never wrote to Anna because he must've seen her fault lines from the first—right through that rug to all the dust beneath. He knew he could play that darkness but couldn't prey on it. She was a mark, a mask. Our family's secrecy was the perfect cover. He slipped right under the rug with us, then pulled it out from under our feet and wrapped a dead body in it.

I'd seen my share of abuse and addiction and mental illness, but I had never seen anything like this. Better the devil you know, that's for sure.

∴

My mother was *always* seeking answers outside of herself, always looking for a savior. Way before David, when Amy was about a year old, Anna made a friend in the neighborhood named Sofia. Sofia was a Greek fortune teller who read my mother's future in the swirled coffee grounds at the bottom of her cup. It was always the stuff she knew my mom would wanna hear: that a tall, dark, handsome man would be showing up soon with lots of money.

They became fast friends.

In fact, for quite some time, Sofia wholly *owned* my mom. She was Anna's guru and guide. If Mom wasn't out drinking, she visited *curandero* shops with Sofia. She'd spend the little bit of money we had on magical candles and sprays, special bottles of holy water, and herbs. She paid Sofia with our food stamps in the hopes that the fortune teller would deliver on promises she had made to send Preston crawling back to Mom.

It became quickly apparent to Sofia that Preston wasn't returning to Anna because of Amy. *The baby is full of demons,* she said, and Amy's temperament didn't help much in convincing Mom otherwise.

So, Mom and Sofia built this large wooden cross one night and dragged it into the house. That thing was probably five feet tall, and they nailed it right to the wall. Mom banished Thovas and me outside but kept Amy in the house as she and Sofia lit rows and rows of candles. I remember Amy's panicked cries over the strange commandments and recitations of Mom and Sofia; as they grew hoarser and more desperate, I couldn't take it anymore. I busted in to find my little sister tethered, upside-down, on the cross. Her diaper was soiled and leaking, her face turning beet red. Mom splashed Amy with holy water as Sofia mumbled strange words.

Amy had been upside-down for too long and was breathing in little whimpers. I rushed to untie her sweaty little body from the cross as Sofia proclaimed that, for interrupting the ritual, it was now *I* who held Satan within. I just carried Amy outside, watching as color returned to her skin.

I clasped her tight and bobbed her up and down, *shh, shh*-ing and telling her it was okay, she was safe. I didn't believe in Satan, but as close to it as it could be, I felt, was within those women inside the house—in the sick power Sofia had over my mother, who allowed it all.

For years, we kids would awaken to find candles and shallow bowls of water with eggs surrounding the area where we slept. We were dragged along to Sofia's house to sit in the living room while she and Mom chanted and whispered spells upon Amy and me, the devil girl children just sitting on the sofa.

∴

After we learned about David, Anna did her own disappearing act. By the time she resurfaced, she'd already moved on, "married" and "divorced" a few more men: a Mormon polygamous doctor who tried to heal her with herbs and hands laid on, and another man, a sweet crossdresser who played up her stylish side.

But something serious had shifted within Anna in her time with David. Maybe Mom's mind hadn't caught on to his doings, but perhaps her spirit did. Her inner antenna caught the signal that something dark needed to be transmuted. This was my mother's mission, the steady eye of her hurricane—the most unspoken thing of her being. Because there were no words for it.

David's allusions to the words of Jesus were perpetual. He spoke them over dinner and repeated them in his letters. Anna, as well, was tight with her saints, as always. I'd thought perhaps their shared sense of devotion was one of the things that brought them together, and maybe it was, on the surface. But David's faith was a front. Perhaps he really believed, but it was in a permission-slip Jesus.

My mother's devotion was something different. She *couldn't* change, and she was as ruthless as David with her fireball rain—but her appeals to a higher power came from a place of pleading. She didn't know how *not* to destroy, but deep within, she wanted to create.

And so she did.

Mom

∴

Anna couldn't stop herself from creating any less than she could from destroying. She was driven to it and not even conscious of why; she just did it.

For pretty much my whole life, Mom made dolls—thousands of them. All that she couldn't see in herself and refused to see in us, Mom put into her dolls. They represented the thing inside her that wanted to mend itself but didn't know how. The dolls ranged in size from about a foot to five feet tall, made of old tapestries and textiles, birds' nests, and threads and ribbons. Bundles of sticks dressed in clothing Anna made herself and hand-embroidered with anatomical hearts. They weren't anything a child would want to play with. They were frightening even, a little: totems, talismans, but not toys.

Mom wasn't gonna sugarcoat anything, not ever. But she also wasn't going to let it pass by. Nothing in her life, it seemed, was salvageable. But *everything* was material.

Once, Anna and I passed a car accident, a bad one. There was shattered windshield glass all over the side of the road, and Mom jerked the wheel onto the shoulder to get out and collect it. Smears of blood smudged up some of the shards, which only made them more beautiful to her. My mother brought these slivers home and glued them to a grotto she'd sculpted, a mosaic of tragedy and triumph—a shelter for her dolls, illuminated by prayer candles.

∴

After David, my mother couldn't stop making these small sanctuaries. Every little discarded thing had a purpose and a place. Broken glass and locks of hair were all part of a story she needed to tell, somehow, since her own narrative was off-limits.

David's darkness had upped the ante on Anna. It startled my mother to a degree that even she wished to carve a bit of light in the world. In addition to the shrines themselves, the little dolls, *retablos*, and *ex-votos* Anna made were the only safe way she could speak of and to the shadows. They were her recognition and her offering—a bit of matter, coated in glitter, and placed before a saint.

Anna reappeared on the southside of San Antonio, bleary from her old rituals within the tabernacles of her beloved *conjunto* bars. It was a spiritual hangover. She couldn't move back into the apartment she'd shared with David, and her dalliances with the whole diversity of men had bombed dramatically. She decided to grow where she was planted and set down roots in that neighborhood.

Mom only knew how to alchemize through her art, and the woman was drawn to an altar. Those little roadside reliquaries that dot the roads in Mexico, tended to by people you never see but who miraculously keep the candles lit inside—nothing in the world moved Anna like these shrines. Only drugs got close, but even they lost their shine.

The Little Grotto Shop grew up in the front room of Anna's new place on Nogalitos Street. It became a haven of protection for neighbors and a steady address for us to visit our mother. The miniature grottoes Anna crafted then were constantly in flux, made and shaped and moved and sold. But the large personal altar she created there stayed, and kept her.

Anna, by Pat Landes

Each morning, Anna awoke early to make a big pot of coffee and get the water boiling in her trusty old bean pot for a big batch of pinto beans. She'd visit her altar and light candles for the Virgin, for Jesus, and all her other saints, Don Pedrito Jaramillo foremost among them. She spoke to each of 'em like they were right there beside her. With her last match, Mom lit a cigarette, headed to the front porch, propped open the screen door, and chatted with passers-by in her broken Spanish. By the afternoon, her home smelled of *comino* and *copal*, coffee, and cigarette smoke. All day, neighbors wandered through this refuge that my mother had created from nothing, for everything.

Every so often, a stray collector would stumble in and amble back to Anna's workroom as though it were some secret hideout. From the inside, the room could've been anywhere, windowless as it was. Lit by a glaring bare bulb hanging from the flat raw-wood ceiling, its turquoise walls vibrated a backdrop of bright desert sky for a surreal selection of crosses amid textiles piled like puffy acid-wash rainclouds. These random connoisseurs would buy up each piece Mom had made or remade. Immediately, she'd scout for more, and on one such outing, she stumbled upon Ray Thurmond.

Ray was a homeless veteran with a soft heart and a shared love of looking for shiny shit on the ground. They bonked heads and fell head-over-heels. It was hard for Ray to be enclosed, but he felt at home inside a room painted like sky. There he hunkered down, helping Anna craft from wood whatever her whirring mind and bleeding heart could imagine. He stayed at her side from that moment on. When they eventually married and she took his last name, they'd sign their initials to each creation: A.R.T.

Sometimes a cactus blooms, and it's the most glorious surprise. Sometimes, there's more than enough water within.

⁖

Mary of Guadalupe was everything to Mom. All that she had ever needed and could not receive, all that she wanted to be but didn't know how. Anna understood Mary's pierced heart, wrapped around and around with thorns, as she understood the absolute beauty and perfect potential in broken things. The image of the Virgin adorns so much of the clothing I create because I believe that that shattered-open heart teaches us all a bit better how to love.

All those years when I'd have to scoop up or step over or seek my mom in alley- ways, every single time she was clinging to a rosary. Plastic, metal, wooden, seeds, or dried roses formed into beads—the material morphed as the rosaries busted or got lost, and Anna gave away as many of them as she found in a forever flow. I'm sure there are still strands circling around out there to this day. It was never a ploy or a prop for her, but her pure humanity beneath and beyond everything.

They say your heart breaks to let the light in, but at some point, some of our hearts break so hard and so often that they're just filled with light, which has no choice but to shine back out. Maybe saints realize that before the rest of us do, which is why they're always pointing to their hearts. They ask us not to harden against but open to. They speak in tongues of trinkets, flowers and beads and glitter, small innocent things that insist throughout even the darkest times—bits of bright that are the philosophers' stone. Strung up and clung to, shapeshifting the world itself.

Chapter 11

CIRCUS

THE HEAVENLY BLUE AND PURPLE MORNING GLORIES AND MUS-
cadine grape vines that climbed the walls and crept into the windows of
mine and Kelly's house on Trail Street had brought in more than ladybugs
and praying mantises. Together, we built a life there. What we painted on
the floors and walls told the story of our youth, our small triumphs, our
awe.

Strangers were drawn to pass by as we, driven and hopeful, constructed
a story. *What is this place?* they asked from rolled-down car windows, and
we shielded our eyes from the sun to extend some explanation.

How does one clarify for others an inner need? For making visible
and tangible the old-soul yearnings of a youth spent anchorless? For rec-
reating those art museum grounds, I had spent nights stowed away upon,
dreaming. It had all come true.

∴

But as with any old house, there were constant repairs. No matter how
good we were at patching things up with Mod Podge and shiplap, the
elements had their way. Neither of us could pause the prolific evolution

that blossomed from every nook of our home and urged us, as individuals, to follow its flourishing.

Growing apart is still growth, and all growth is a little painful.

The universe issued its ultimatum in big red letters: NOTICE. An official intimation stuck in the frame of the front screen door spelled it out. Kelly and I had weeks to collect our things and vacate the premises. Our landlord was selling. Losing the house on Trail Street meant that Kelly and I had to face the fact that while we'd be forever family and forever friends, our romantic relationship no longer had a container.

Sometimes, you gotta actually see things get bulldozed to the ground to accept that they're changing. The morning of our home's demolition, the bulldozer crew waited for us as we wrangled our outdoor cats. Then, with an all-clear signal, the leveling began.

My brain grasped the process, but damn if my heart didn't feel like the wreckage before my eyes. Kelly and I sat close on his truck's tailgate and cried. All I could do was cling to the cat in my lap, her frightened form swaddled in a scratchy towel. I soothed her stunned little shudders and watched it all fall down.

⁂

Kelly's truck had been my rescue wagon and my ambulance. That day, it served as a vehicle in a different sense, as a means of passage. Our dream home and my childhood sweetheart were both now in the rearview, and I was only nineteen.

There was some joke my dad used to tell me about the difference between optimism and pessimism. A guy takes his two sons, one a pessimist and one an optimist, to a room full of horse shit. The first kid is really pissed, but the optimist kid jumps right in, sure there's a pony in there somewhere.

As I watched Kelly drive away, I didn't know where to begin again. I was scraping the bottom of the barrel of my heart, just as tired as could be. I needed something new and different, some sparkly pony behind all the shit. I looked through the want ads in the back of the paper with tears in my eyes, hungry for something—I knew not what.

In the teensiest print, so small I had to wipe my eyes and hold the paper right up to my nose, was an ad offering private clowning lessons from a retired Barnum and Bailey clown. The address was right in my neighborhood and totally up my alley, and I knew just what I needed to do.

∴

The carnie genes are strong in me; the masquerade of the circus colors everything I see. It's neither purely fantasy nor complete reality, but a bit of both. The first actual dress I ever designed when I was about three years old, with the help of my Grandmother Brown on a trip back to Texas, was a fun polka-dot number. It was supposed to be for Easter, but the pattern brought me to the circus, where I figured Jesus worked. I wore that thing over my little boxer shorts every day, flying on the back of the Triumph.

Clowns had the magic and the love. And the shoes. Clown shoes are really the ultimate in footwear. The very best ones are made in Italy. I don't remember how I came to know this—from a young age, I was just so interested in all aspects of clowning, tip to toe.

High Pockets the Clown answered his door wearing a starched-thin white button-down tucked into khaki pants, which, somewhat disappointingly, were neatly rolled up atop a pair of sensible street shoes. He was tall and string-bean lanky, a little stooped with age. Calliope clown music blasted my face, riding on the air of a window unit A/C that also carried the scent of freshly popped popcorn.

For a second, I figured I was about to be kidnapped. I'd just spent months cluelessly getting chummy with a deranged serial killer; maybe I should pay a little better attention. But High Pockets put me instantly at ease, offering me a little red-and-white-striped bag of popcorn and inviting me to sit with a few other clown hopefuls on his threadbare tweed couch.

I was enchanted. His whole place was a miniature circus museum. Stripes and glitter, huge sunglasses, and spangled stars shone from every cranny of his pocket-sized apartment. Barnum and Bailey posters hung on each wall—framed photographs of High Pockets on stilts wearing eight-foot-long striped pajamas and a pointy clown hat, posing with other notable clowns and circus performers.

High Pockets sat serious and poised, straight-backed across from us in his recliner.

I'm just gonna tell you the truth, he said naked-face matter-of-fact; *most people don't make it past the first screening. So please don't be disappointed; I'm real finicky about who gets through. I'm an old man now and don't have much energy to invest.*

And no gum chewing.

∴

He had a bit of crotchety sternness, but High Pockets was a big, tall softy. He was like a barometer for clown spirit. He knew it right away if your heart wasn't in the right place.

I visited High Pockets in his maudlin music-box apartment three times a week for about a year. We'd sit in front of a smudgy vanity mirror caking on oily face paint as he taught me the basics of makeup and expression. In his sunbaked treeless parking lot, I learned to walk on stilts. Together, we'd hop into his big brown Oldsmobile sedan, all decked out and done up in our clown garb, polka-dot trousers brushing against the velour seats and frizzed neon wigs smooshing the droopy fabric ceiling. Trying not to sweat our makeup off on the road to some community center or children's hospital.

I imagined what people in traffic thought of us. I hoped it brought a smile to their day.

∴

My dad was an avid news watcher. One evening, spacing out over a bowl of Cheerios, he saw a ragtag clown troupe putting on a show at a local mall. I don't know how he picked me out of the lineup, but he did. I hadn't even told him about it because it was something that was all mine, and I didn't wanna hear anything negative about it.

It's a funny thing to be confronted about your closet clown life. I fessed up, of course. I had assumed that as soon as I was a bona fide, card-carrying Barnum and Bailey clown, I could drop in on the circus whenever it scuttled through Central Texas. But Preston brought it home that clowning of the kind I was pursuing wasn't just a hobby. I'd be committed to a life of traveling with the circus—leaving school and my family to follow this path, and did I really want to do that?

It popped my entire balloon. I wasn't down to clown, after all. It was like the big-top collapsed, and everything packed up and disappeared overnight. I went to High Pockets and told him about my decision, and he nearly cried in his popcorn. He was an expressive clown but a reserved man. That little tear in his eye was a big thing, and tough to see.

I never saw or spoke to High Pockets again after that day, but my experience with him is one of the greatest gifts of my life. It might have saved my life.

∴

I was twenty years old and didn't know how to punctuate a sentence properly.

I'd always relied on little tricks to do the things I loved. Sidestepped the measurements and saw the patterns in an inside-out visual language. I slogged through each beloved book so slowly as though I were reading the author's lips. Sitting to study was like trying to smoosh together two magnets with the same polarity—I wanted the subject matter to click, but it all slid around. Math, especially, felt emotional and dizzying.

Since I couldn't join the circus, I decided to try going back to school. That year, a special Presidential grant through the Clinton administration allowed poor kids like me to go to college, so I rode my bike down to San Antonio College to register. Turns out, no matter how I paid for it, I couldn't enroll until I completed some remedial classes; aptitude tests told me and my counselor I was dyslexic and learning disabled. My writing was terrible. My comprehension of mathematics was abysmal.

The swirling subject matter was one thing. What was worse was the chatter in my mind. I could hear Preston saying, *Kid, they're just gonna brainwash you.* And the voice of my mother: *Imposter.*

I was challenging the idea that I was unteachable. The idea that I was unlovable. I was observing my mind's workings gently. My counselor encouraged me to take time with the subject matter. There was no rush, no bear chasing me to the end of each paragraph. I had to allow myself to slow down, which proved more difficult than anything.

∴

I decided I was gonna train for the motherfuckin' Tour de France. I wasn't messing around; I got a thrift store bike, fixed it all up, and rode for miles, fast, around San Antonio.

Only one person could keep up with me. Robert was a 1980s version of James Dean who went to Trinity University and drove a fancy car. He was tan and fit and smart—he could do anything and wanted to teach me everything. He was like MacGyver mixed with Henry Higgins from *My Fair Lady*, and I was his perfect Eliza Doolittle, complete with flowers in my hair and a shaky hold on proper English.

I had crooked teeth, and I didn't know how to drive a car. Robert paid for me to get braces and put me in the front seat. I fell head over heels in love.

Muscle and Fitness magazine was Robert's bible. I'd thumb through the pages in awe of the women in there. They were superheroes. No one was gonna hurt them—no one would even dare try. So, I took up weightlifting alongside Robert. He pushed me and encouraged me. Heavier and heavier, harder and harder. I joined the lifting team at San Antonio College and earned piles of trophies, each topped with a bronze goddess, strong as shit and bright as the sun.

That first year with Robert was more fun than I'd ever had—each moment like a hit of speed that made my everyday hustle seem manageable: work, school, lifting, cycling, family.

Little by little, my system became addicted.

∴

It's easy to see when someone's life is run by drugs. The paraphernalia is inescapable. When the hook is another human, it's trickier to spot. Though I didn't touch drugs, with Robert, I experienced highs never before imagined. And I thought I knew lows, but there are forever deeper depths.

His taunts that began in the gym spread and bled into every aspect of my being. My form was goofy, and the weights were skimpy. He got me braces only after making fun of my mouth and taught me to drive after ridiculing my reliance on a bike. Only when he sowed a seed of doubt within would Robert water me. Before I knew it, a garden of insecurity had sprung up in my soul—a flower from each little wound, blood red. Instead of seeing them as warning flags, my unconscious followed 'em like landing beacons, signaling me back to a familiar place. I was lulled and dragged—Dorothy from *The Wizard of Oz* passing out in a field of poppies.

His teasing turned to screaming, to hitting, to maiming. It was a roller coaster I knew well, but still, I threw my arms up and my head back and whooped to the heavens. Sick to my belly when it shuddered to a halt, I'd get right back in line and do it all again. I shrugged off the signal flares as fireworks. *This was just how relationships went.*

For four years, Robert and I stayed together. Schooled in silence and shame, I didn't tell a soul about the abuse. I couldn't even be honest with myself about it. A horrific car accident in childhood had left him with head trauma. This fact endeared him to me—the gorgeous golden boy at my side was broken and in pain. It wasn't his fault, and I knew I could love it all away and fix him.

There were multiple rock bottoms—times Robert beat the shit out of me and screamed in my face, then sped away in his sports car. And I'd run right after him, no matter the weather, shoeless and snot-faced and begging him to return. I honestly believed I'd die if he didn't come back. It's humiliating to admit, and it's taken years and years for me to have compassion around that. Even so, I still wanna go back in time and shake the shit out of that version of me. You can't fix the past, but that's *exactly* what I was trying to do then—chasing down Anna all over again.

I'd just white-knuckle my way through it, down to the bone.

∴

The fight that ended everything began like nothing. I don't even remember what it was about. But suddenly, Robert snapped. The force of his rage, honed by heavy weights, flew at me in fists and feet. The encounter left me with broken teeth and ribs, my body pancaked into the ground in our front yard, where I'd hit the deck as he leveled a shotgun at me. He'd missed and punctured the tire of the car he'd gifted me and left just like that.

The screech of his wheels driving away lurched at my old-habit heart, the voice in my head like an antique doll's warbled voicebox, *No, stop, come back.* But another voice rang louder, steadier—the same angelic tone that had comforted me as a child when Mom beat me. It sat me down, looked me in the eyes, and said, *Robin, what the fuck are you doing?*

If I could have compassion for my mother, I could surely scrape some together for myself.

∴

Just as when I was a baby, my first step in standing back up was to detox.

Recovery from an abusive relationship mimics the withdrawal from heroin or alcohol. Though I had chosen life, I thought about suicide often at that time. I adjusted my focus every five minutes, absorbed only with what was right before my face. I knew I needed to stay away from Robert to stay alive. But he'd come sniffing back, and I'd drop everything. He'd show up at my door and ask me to ride with him to the Poteet Strawberry Festival, and the only thing I could say was, *Lemme get my backpack!* I took everything as a divine sign that we were meant to continue, but really, it was just another hit.

I was stuck, spiraling, and then Robert got busted on some random charge. Turns out he had a past rap sheet of prior assaults and drugs, and he was put away for seven years. As David, the serial killer, had done, Robert sent stacks of letters—proclaiming his love, apologizing. Sometimes I responded, sometimes I didn't.

Before all the violence had begun, Robert had gifted me his old 1969 Dodge Dart—the one whose tire he'd shot out. In our happier days, he and I'd painted the whole exterior with cheetah spots and psychedelic zebra stripes, ripped off the doors and gone for windy joy rides around town.

I drove around San Antonio in that thing for about six years, adding new little details with the miles. Friends put their stamps and stickers upon it, and it brought smiles to all I sat among in traffic. It was my vehicle of healing. My own personal clown car.

⁘

A child will not go where it does not feel safe. And sometimes, the least safe space of all is in your own mind. Maybe you can't be positive or hopeful, but you can at least try to be gentle.

*I'd wanted to become a clown because I wanted to be part of something that provides that kind of safe space for children and the inner child in each of us. The space where it feels like someone is on your side, even if that person looks ridiculous. **Especially** if they look ridiculous.*

From the start, there's so much pressure to conform to some impossible ideal of having it all together, of looking and moving and behaving in a certain perfect way. And that's the most laughable thing of all. Beneath the makeup and the masks, and the muscles, we're just molecules doing magic math. It's tragic how we treat each other from the places of our pain, but it's a true miracle if we can even get a glimpse of how we might heal ourselves and help others.

Clowning is an obedience to a spirit that honors the whole spectrum of what we share. Every piece of clothing I've ever made has a sprinkle of this spirit within—the sublime silliness required to take life seriously, the little bit of wonder that's in each of us. At the end of the day, it's a big circus, a grand parade. We're all in it together, bare-assed in clown suits.

Chapter 12

EYES

WHAT I'D STRUGGLED MOST WITH IN CLOWN SCHOOL WERE those damn balloon animals. Instead of skipping over it, High Pockets had me stand there with multicolored worms of spent balloons at my feet, struggling with the squeaky, misshapen snakes and swords that were the best offering my fumble-fingers could make. It wasn't some weird clown torture; it was the entire point.

Kids could see that and understand. They get that magic doesn't always happen as you want it to, but they still believe in it. Somewhere along the line, we start to worry more about what people think of us instead of what we were born to create with our own hands, our own breath. But the child in us still wants to believe in that fulfillment, even if others call us clowns.

After my time with High Pockets, I came down from my stilts and sat on the floor with kids—got a child development certificate, and started working at a school in San Antonio nestled right inside the park where I'd spent so many nights in my homeless days. Teaching children to swim in the same spot where Preston had taught me felt like a surreal full-circle experience. And if felt full. I felt full. And then, for better or worse, I fell in love again.

∴

John had been a friend who'd held the dustpan as I swept up the pieces of my heart after Robert. As I sat with children, he took over the operations at the other end of the telescope, working with the elderly at his family's retirement center a few miles away in Pleasanton. I'd visit sometimes to hang out and help out, but each time I left, it was with a lump of sadness in my belly. The place was falling apart, and the residents needed more love and care than they were receiving. Returning to my work at the school was dizzying, pinballing between the viewpoints that see life from the beginning and the end, opening and closing. It was an honor to sit with all these teachers, young and old.

I said yes when John invited me to live with him in Pleasanton, in an army bunker behind the retirement center. I wanted to make the whole place warm, to bring a sense of lightness and joy—that High Pockets and the children had schooled me in, that I'd clung to through my worst days in my most challenging years—to this place full of people who had so much to share and deserved the best care.

I stayed for a decade.

∴

I had official jobs at the center: administering medication and managing scripts and doses. I cooked the residents' food, brought them their meals, and cleaned like my mom would walk in drunk any minute. It filled my cup to fill everyone else's, as literally as I did so a million times a day, into Styrofoam tumblers trembling from arthritis-swollen fingers. I brought in animals—a pet for each resident if they were into it. Rescue cats and birds, mainly.

The radio was on at all times and I danced through everything for a while—giggling with the old ladies in chair aerobics, brushing their wispy tumbleweed hair and glittering their cracked fingernails. I'd sit on the edge of their beds late into the night, rubbing liniments into their aching hands and talking over tea and graham crackers as Looney Toons bubbled on in the background. It was like having twenty-seven grandparents, and I loved every one of them.

I hadn't experienced much death up to that point. Though I'd grown up in a family forever on the edge, we'd always landed on our feet and had nine lives each, at least. I thought I'd get used to the death part of the job at the retirement center, but as time drew on, the loss of each resident hit me like a rock-salt slug to the heart. How many times I laid flat on the tile floor of John's office, crying on the phone to my dad. I wanted my father to say the right thing to fix it all, but as is the case with heartbreaking truths, the best-case-scenario advice is simply to endure it. To recognize the suffering and do what you can to ease it.

Hang in there, kid, he said. *Give those old people all you can in the way only you can.*

∴

Sometimes families came for their loved ones' things after they died, and sometimes they just didn't. Each quilt or doily left behind somehow found its way into our bunker. It was an entire inheritance. A woman at the center had gifted me her old Singer sewing machine in her last days; I set it up at our kitchen table and stayed up late ripping and reattaching these scraps left behind. It was all I could do to make sense of the loss overflowing as the wire baskets surrounded my feet, gushing with handkerchiefs and lace gloves, stained handmade aprons with names embroidered upon the hem, and torn bits of wedding clothes. Some nights, I fell asleep right there with my head on the table, drooling on piles of linen and heaps of nubby cotton nightgowns.

I thought I was the only person in the world who liked what I made, and that was fine with me—I made pieces for and from sheer life force. But sometimes, I'd sell the things I made from all those mismatched materials: first, to friends of friends who I figured were just being nice. Then, stuff started happening in parking lots. I'd find women following me. Not fanatically or scarily, just hovering on my periphery, smiling, eventually asking, *Where did you get that?* I'd respond with a mix of bashfulness and something like pride. It felt nice, and it was maybe the first time I let myself be OK with that feeling—not from a person or a prize, but from something I had made with my own two hands, bringing a little instance of joy in the middle of a parking lot.

I clung to those glimpses as much as I did each penny earned from whatever pieces I might have sold. Money was beyond tight, robbing Peter to pay Paul *and* Mary and writing hot checks for groceries. Those crazy mended bloomers and repurposed slips patched the leak sometimes, but as the years went on, there was less and less time to devote to clothing-making. No one in my sphere supported it, anyway. My "silly little craft."

There was so much work to do—too much. Most nights, I slept on a thin little plastic mat on the floor at the facility, then up way before the sun to eat a bowl of plain oatmeal, usually my only meal for the day. I kept trying to stick to my dad's advice—to consider my job there as though I was in a sort of ashram, a warrior training camp for the soul. I knew there are times in life that are just about putting one foot in front of the other. Desert times, mining times, plain-ass-oatmeal-every-day times.

But your body doesn't have a poker face. Years of taking care—of my family, my boyfriends, and more—had taken a toll. The residents looked at me with genuine worry. *What are you doing,* they asked, *spending your young life here taking care of us?*

Get out of here, girl, they said, *Go.*

∴

Behind the bunker John and I called home, ran acres and acres of undeveloped scrubland. It was a vista to stare at in the heat until your eyes reverberated with mirages, resonating with all that emptiness. My mental chatter droned on like the cicadas cranking in their own sort of relay.

But there was a tree, a 350-year-old oak that was one of the oldest in the county.

I'd shuffle out there like a zombie and put my forehead to its trunk, trying to will its wisdom into my brain. What had it seen that it could share with me? All *I* could see were those wavy heat lines for miles, a place for people to dump puppies and old couches, a place where people came to die.

Rock bottom is a fine place for a clown, but it's all wrong for a caretaker.

I'd given and given until my giving became taking. I was no longer bringing comfort; I was bringing concern.

That tree didn't grow for me or for anyone. It did so for its own glory. And how.

∴

There's so much power in a woman traveling alone of her own volition, no matter how old or where she's going. It shows the world that no matter what you tell me about myself, I'm still here, and I want to see more life.

I'd read about a place in Florida in the back of some old hippie magazine: a holistic healing center named for Hippocrates that taught nutrition and natural medicine. Fuck it. I wrote them one day, applied for a scholarship, and got it. I have no idea how, and I'll always wonder, but at the time, I was more freaked out at the prospect of going.

I didn't know what to do with what was a windfall of fortune for me. I'd have to scrape together airfare and traveling money. It was forever my M.O. to allocate each extra cent I made to my family; my inner calculator was constantly tabulating food for us, balancing Mom and Dad's caffeine and nicotine budget, rent and gas and disaster. Maybe, for the first time, I was showing the universe I was *at least* as valuable as a can of Folgers and a pack of smokes. I had to figure how John would run the retirement center in my absence, how my dad would manage the distance, and if my mom would survive my trip at all.

Anna and I hadn't been super close since I moved to Pleasanton. She was busy at her Grotto Shop and with her husband, Ray, who sometimes wandered out to sleep under the freeway because it's where he felt he could breathe. She was on and off the wagon and really just falling apart. Her health was *bad* bad. She'd had back surgery to fix a disc, and her body went septic after the operation. She was in the ICU in San Antonio, in and out of consciousness as they tried to de-poison my mother.

If I went to Florida, I might never see Anna alive again.

When I visited her in the hospital and saw her lying there in a sedated haze, tubes running from her body to a machine and back again, maybe for a single moment, I wished she'd snap right awake and tell me to stay. It was second nature for me to go down with her ship, sometimes easier to sink. I was just drained enough to consider it. But this time, there was land in sight. It meant facing a lot of shit I was terrified of—flying, leaving. Myself.

I prayed to bless and protect Anna, told her I loved her, and hoped she's be there when I got back. The guilt ate my lunch all the way to Florida—I might as well have bought it a seat.

∴

Still, I landed. Stepped out of the plane in silver sparkle sneakers. If I was going to heal, it would look like this: a real metamorphosis.

Except for when we lived in California, I hadn't traveled anywhere in my twenty-five years and didn't know how to pack, aside from the clothes on my back and Mom's bean pot. So, for my trip to Florida, I brought every piece of clothing I owned. As long as they weren't scrubs, they were stuffed in the suitcase—all the starry sanity-saving garb I could grab.

I sewed stars onto everything: pants, jackets, shoes, dresses. I got the habit from my father, who'd forever doodled the heavens in the margins of my life—scribbled Saturns and stars upon stars upon stars. When I missed him, which was always, I'd add a star to whatever I was working on. I felt comfortable in the clothing I made, threaded from scraps of stolen time, from left-behind beloved bits, sewn with every bit of hope I could muster. More than that, I felt safe. It wasn't a suit of armor; it was my insides on the outside—a wearable prayer. Classmates asked me what I was doing studying natural medicine, curious why I wasn't pursuing fashion. I thought to myself that was a dream for another lifetime.

We were encouraged at Hippocrates to make vision boards—those collages with images cut from catalogs and magazines glued onto the kind of drug-store poster board kids use for science projects. You paste your ideal future on them so your eyes can see. For a moment, I felt ridiculous. Who was I to believe I deserved to dream, much less to think it might come true? I called bullshit on those boards.

I made them anyway. I covered every inch with cut-out kittens and bouquets of printed roses, plants and hearts, and hippie-hopeful words like "peace" and "dream." It was a backdrop for future clothing designs, a hodgepodge of simple and sincere hope.

∴

Hippocrates was the first to say that illnesses weren't a punishment inflicted by the gods. Years of being told the devil himself lived in me and needed to be beaten out—my brain knew it was bullshit, but back home, I'd been treating myself like it was true. "Physician, heal thyself" was one of the central maxims at the Institute. I'd been sticking Bugs Bunny Band-Aids over arrow wounds for years; I had a lot of work to do.

I spent four months at the Institute, in classes six days a week, from sunup to sundown. Making medicine, preparing food, and reading books late into the night. Still, each evening, I found myself sitting in the main lobby, tied to the telephone. It was an open-air kind of foyer, set up like the community hub of a tropical hostel. Cross-legged on the Saltillo tile floor, watching the bougainvilleas and papaya trees shifting hues with the sunset, I'd wait on hold for whichever night nurse was on duty watching over my mom. I knew each of those women's names, and each day, their report was the same: Anna was holding steady but still unresponsive. Calls to Preston and John were likewise one-way conversations—both of them still pretty annoyed with me for taking the leap.

I knew if I hadn't, my spirit at least would have ceased. Saving ourselves sometimes means hurting others, even if only in small ways, even if only temporarily. It's mercy math: there's a cost, but we count, too. I wasn't used to inserting my own needs into the equation in such a clear way, and it all felt foreign and bewildering as fuck. I did the only thing I knew to do, diving into the clothes I had brought and decking myself out in the pieces that made me feel happiest: holey Levi's with stars sewn and drawn all over, a flowing patched tunic from an old lady's nightgown set, embroidered with flowers and cosmos: polka-dot socks and silver glitter Vans. I stuck bright red hibiscus flowers into my messy braids.

And then I went to the mall.

∴

I'd been inside a mall exactly once, in my clowning days with High Pock-ets—at his side in the echoey atrium, wrestling with those balloons. I liked the big fountain they'd propped up in the middle and how people of all ages tossed penny-wishes into it.

I'd never seen such a place as this mall in Florida; as I made my way through the parking lot filled with real Rolls-Royces and people in yacht-ing clothes, I felt those eyes again.

The woman I met in the parking lot that day owned a store in the mall. She was sweet, an older hippie wearing strands of amber and sandalwood oil. She looked like a poet. On the spot, she asked if I'd made my clothing, and when I said, *Yes*, she handed me her card. *Bring whatever you've got whenever you can*, she said. Good thing I'd overpacked.

I hoofed it back to my little room at Hippocrates and crammed everything I'd brought into my duffel. I kept my bathing suit, busted-out Birkenstocks, board shorts, and a ratty-painted cloud T-shirt—my uniform when I returned to the mall and for the rest of my time in Florida. Instead of a business card, that day, the shop owner-poet handed me a check. She bought every last late-night tear-stained piece I'd made.

Keep making things, she said.

And stay in touch.

∴

I washed my uniform in the little bathroom sink each night, then hung the pieces out in the tropical air. They never really got dry, but I didn't mind. I could wear that beach bum outfit every day for the rest of my life if it meant I could make art that made people happy.

I was so excited that day I got the check from the poet—bowled over. I went straight back to the lobby and called up John, bubbling on about it all. I'd been paid real money! People who could afford yachting clothes were bonkers over my spray-painted shoes and appliquéd vests.

And while he was pleased about the sale, John couldn't see it. I had binoculars, but he was wearing blinders. He was at the helm of a sinking ship, struggling with the retirement center. He was happy for me, but there was just so much sea.

You should never turn your back on the ocean or a dream. Maybe it wasn't the time to push it, but I wouldn't let it go. I had a knowing, and I was falling in love with something just over the horizon. I could lower the volume on my vision to a whisper and keep it near—the ocean sound in a seashell—waiting for the right time to put it to my ear.

∴

I finished my studies. I earned my certificate. I was flying home to Texas with a duffel bag much lighter in all respects but filled with medicine. It was right back into the blender, bittersweet. As soon as my stinky Birkenstocks hit the pavement, I was drawn to work. But before that, I needed to see Anna.

How many times had I visited her like this? So many hospital hallways by heart. The very day I landed, Mom was transferred from ICU. Semilucid and drugged, as she'd be every single day from that point forward. But she could speak.

I pushed open the heavy hospital door to find her sitting up, talking to her husband, Ray. He smiled at the sight of me, and Anna flopped her head in my direction. Squinty and scratchy-voiced, the first words I heard her speak in months were,

Where the fuck have you been?

∴

My navy blue scrubs were hanging right where I'd left 'em. As I pulled their plain cotton back on, I was determined not to let them wear me this time.

I tried out everything in my new arsenal—had the folks at the home making fuckin' vision boards and doing guided meditations every chance I got. They weren't big fans of me emerging from the kitchen with carrot bran muffins instead of chocolate chip cookies. I worked to restore the garden, but the heat had its way. Every morning, I walked out to the big oak, and every night, I sat at my sewing machine in the bunker, talking to God. Something had to change, but until it did, I'd just keep making things and staying in touch.

∴

Since childhood, I've always kept a collection of old spectacles around. Dainty horn-rimmed lenses that perch like finches on your nose bridge, big fat Marine-issued "birth-control specs," and round-as-suns peepers like John Lennon wore. Like magic kaleidoscopes into another's viewpoint, they morph what's in front of you and make you remember that we all see shit differently.

It's such elemental magic to recall that you're the only one who sees things from your particular vision. Even if we don't have sight, that inner canvas of colors at their most basic, imagined fractals of broken light is an in-vision we all carry, an invitation to create what we see.

When no one else believes in you, you gotta depend on what your inner eye is focusing on. Showing up for yourself causes the universe to adjust to your vision. A big printed eye on the middle of a T-shirt might not seem like much magic, but it speaks the wisdom of your heart, which knows things before the mind.

It draws in spirits with the same prescription.

Between the beginning and the end, we're all telescopes, connecting the world with our eyes squinched toward the wonder: outside of us, within us, all of us, together.

Memorize all that you love.
Gather it in your memory.
Close your eyes and Replay it often.
Like films
Like music
Return whenever
and however
you are called.
Let this become
your Rhythm

Let this be
your home.

Chapter 13

RAW HEMS

YOU COULDN'T QUITE SEE IT, BUT JUST BEHIND OUR BUNKER, beyond the big oak and past those vacant acres of swaying grasses, snuggled in a stand of mesquites, stood a home—a falling-down rock house that was probably a hundred years old. Just a shell with no roof or furnishings and a dirt floor. All those living rooms Dad and I had arranged in junkyards years earlier would've looked so badass in that crumbling space, and he joined me there often to dream.

He and I had worn a path through the grass like a snaking river, run alongside by our new sidekick, Humphrey. Humphrey was a mutt I'd been led to by a particular resident of the center who was prone to pointing out small miracles: a bird's nest with eggs in it, a lizard changing colors, a pile of puppies in a field. That dog was the first animal I knew I could protect, and he protected me right back.

Humphrey would chase grasshoppers and get swallowed up by those grasses, his shaggy black form a playful shadow. He'd bring us sticks to throw, and if the weather was okay for a fire, Dad and I would find some of our own. Before we set them to blaze, we scribbled prayers upon their wood with whatever drawing materials Dad brought. We watched their intentions rise with the smoke that met the stars peeking out one by one.

These provisions and practices had sustained us through some shit: a grounding and a reaching.

I was done at the retirement center. A beloved resident named Geraldine, who'd been there for years, had passed away on her birthday minutes after she'd blown out her candle on her Duncan Hines vanilla cake. All Geraldine had in the world was a parrot I had found for her, a sun conure named Sam. She'd always shared her sweets with Sam, and the second I saw the cake's blue and yellow icing smudged upon his beak and little toenails, that was it for me, man. It broke my heart right down. I'd cleaned up Geraldine and thrown my arms around her, kissed her on the cheeks, and whispered, *Happy Birthday,* and *thank you.*

⁙

Soon after Geraldine died, Dad made a special trip down to Pleasanton, stopping by the convenience store to load up on our favorite brownies and fill up his thermos with coffee. We sat in that rock house for hours that night. The primary prayer Preston and I shared, which flew through the open roof to find its place in the heavens, was to live next door to each other in Bandera, on the banks of the Medina River. We'd make art and start a little gallery.

The river was my father's sacred place. He was drawn to it as though he thirsted. It was his idyll, his soul's home. He knew everything about the Medina River—its tributaries, its habits, and its history. It was once the boundary between Texas and Mexico, and this amazed him most of all—how lines get drawn and redrawn throughout the span of one's life. All these arbitrary designations, the limits they describe to divide us. The only real boundary is our own skin. You can only trust where you're drawn, where your love flows.

Whenever Dad swapped his white Hanes V-neck tees for long-sleeved flannels, and it wasn't even cold out, I knew he was using again. It was this inverse spiritual thing. In many religions, when you enter a place of worship, you cover yourself: your body, your head. My father's places of worship were short-sleeved serving in the heat or shirtless in the creek.

This was where his heart shone. Long sleeves showed me he was outside the temple, further from the heart, and in need of protection.

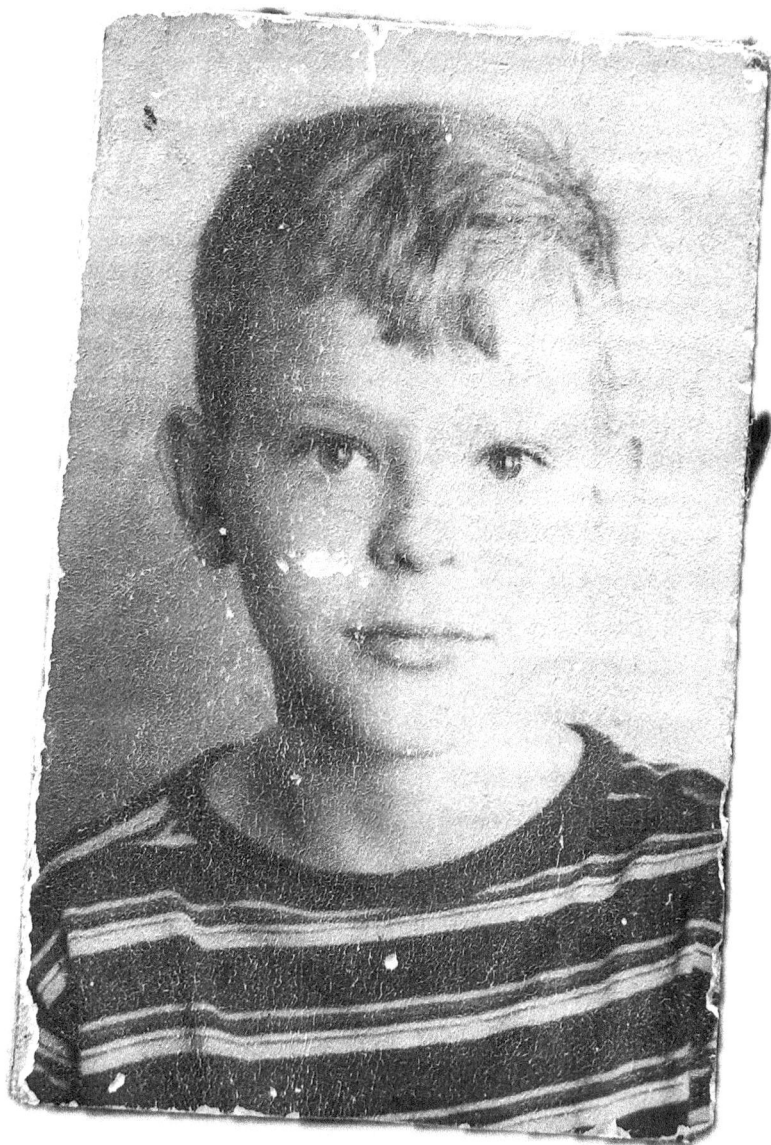

Dad in 4th Grade

Preston knew he didn't have to puncture his skin to sail beyond it. He'd meditated and breathed healing back into his form after the fire. But the pain had stayed. The opiates they prescribed him to manage it over the years courted and hooked him, over and over.

He was fifty-eight, and I was thirty-two in that year, 1996. We were adults who'd been through everything together, but he was ashamed as he rolled up his sleeves to reveal the track marks running over his forearms— evidence of this never-ending catch and release. He asked me not to tell my brother. He said, *Please, I'm just humiliated about it.*

And I just said, *Dad, I love you.*

I held his hand as we walked back to the bunker that night, a shiny silver moon illuminating Humphrey's inky coat as he dipped in and out of the grasses. Between drags of his cigarette, Dad told me the story of Brigadoon, a mythical village in the Scottish Highlands. Placed under a spell and stuck in time, Brigadoon is invisible to the rest of the world except for one day every hundred years. On this day, outsiders can visit and even stay if they love someone in Brigadoon enough to give up the world outside.

When I die, meet me at Brigadoon, Dad half-laughed over his shoulder. *I'll be at the front waiting for you.*

∴

Back in San Antonio, I held Preston's shaking hands in the parking lot of the methadone clinic. Inside, we put his name on the list. The waiting room was like purgatory, souls dizzy in the swing of addiction even as they sat stock-still. We left before his name was called.

I drove Dad back to his house, where he instructed me to leave him be for a few days. Not to call or come by. To let the dope sickness do its thing until he came out the other side. This wasn't the first time. Until I was dismissed from Dad's school of life, I had this mission: Preston was here to teach me lessons, and I would take care of him. I never knew any other way. It never felt like a burden to me because it just felt very real.

A few weeks on, Preston called me. He was brighter, baby-wide-eyed, ready to go out into the world. There was never a time or place that wasn't remarkable with my father—even with him at less than 100 percent, even on a small tour to the drainage ditch at the end of his street. The site was an eyesore, really—stuffed with trash and stagnant old rain, overrun with weeds. But the birds in the area fucking loved it, and Dad and I carried binoculars like we were on some grand expedition.

He'd brought a garbage bag to pick up litter, a servant's heart still beating in his smack-battered frame. As he bent for each beer bottle and glass shard, I saw him weeping. Dad was like a little bird himself out there, learning to fly again. Again and again, his refrain, *It's just so beautiful, kid.* He was frustrated that other people couldn't see what he saw in this overlooked patch of Earth that collects all we discard.

With a trash bag full, we walked back to his house along the railroad tracks, our preferred route. At his home, I put away the litter we had collected and made his bed with freshly washed Star Wars sheets. I held his hand as he drifted into an afternoon nap, kissed his head, and went home.

∴

To his forever credit, within months of Geraldine's death, John found a buyer for the retirement center. There were a million threads to tie and untie in handing over ownership, and letting go completely was a slow release that would take years. We were there, and we weren't, surrounded by death while on the cusp of new life. I wasn't quite sure what to dream about, aside from living next to Dad. The only way I knew to surge forward, even an increment, was to sew.

An endless cycle of the residents' relics—old nightgowns and handkerchiefs reconfigured and reimagined a thousand ways—fed beneath the foot of my machine. Like a child running through an open daffodil field, zigzagging ric-rac this way and that. I reached out to two local seamstresses, Pleasanton natives who ran competing businesses and talked endless shit about each other. I'd ping-pong between their kitchens, which were exactly the same—fabric cast over dining room chairs and tables, coffee brewing. I lugged my ribbons and a bag of cut stars back and forth between them like a silly constellation.

I spent a lot of time alone in the rock house. It felt like my heart, a crumbling and open threshold.

Lying on my back upon the dirt floor, I watched the clouds morph and clear, the elegant fingers of the mesquites swaying into view, their twisted trunks spiraling skyward, aching toward expansion but set still and solid in the dry soil, digging, withstanding—at the suggestion of life itself, who planted the seed, saying, *More of this.*

⁘

The retirement center had been a place for people to come at the end of their journey here on planet Earth. That station isn't a useless stop, not even a little bit. Humans at every point on the path have so much to contribute and teach, so much space and hands to hold—the dying especially so. We'll all get there someday; listening to those on the threshold is an honor, but you gotta get past the fear.

I'd gotten an opportunity to lead art therapy groups at an experimental cancer treatment facility in Southern California. I would work with women who'd been through all the chemo and radiation they could handle, parts of their holy bodies scooped out and sutured up in a quest to extend existence even a few months. All their faces were knowing and serene, with knit caps and shawls spun like frosting upon their heads.

On that cusp, these women were allowing doctors and therapists to try their hand at things that could maybe help them and those who came after them. For three weeks, I helped untangle their hearts' threads through drawing, painting, and creating—the only real "cure" I know.

I told them to paint what their pain felt like, what their disease looked like. And then I told them to draw their healing, whatever that meant to them—the colors. Just take a color and draw a circle, a stick figure; it doesn't matter. It could be very abstract. Draw a picture of yourself—your face, your hands, any part of yourself. And then, I wanted everyone to draw a picture of their heart. One woman used a fat black marker to draw her heart, and she died within days.

I walked to the beach then and sat on the shore. Though the center was nice and clean, the nearest beach was gray and smelled awful. Oil and plastic and sewage combined. The sea air hit your face like a fat slap. I thought of Preston in the drainage ditch, of all the pollution we learn. All we stuff away until it turns our system toxic, the endless work of cleaning it up, restoring things to their beauty. I curled into myself on the shore, shedding tears and snot onto my knees. Because I chose to work at this place for three measly weeks, my father had refused to speak to me.

∴

I can count on one hand the times I've stood up to Preston in my life, but this digit was the biggest. To him, it was a big ole' middle finger. Despite all the times he'd opened the world to me and my eyes to the world, engaging in epic conversations about the unknowable mysteries of existence, this matter was shut tight. The conversation was over. A sudden click signaled the end—the only time he ever hung up on me.

My father wanted to empower and inspire the people around him: *directly* around him. The everyday anchored him. As much as he loved the wide-open Pacific Ocean and the pristine Medina River, my father was just as content to visit that drainage ditch down the street. He'd insisted I was running away; what I needed to do was sit still and stay put. Meditation would give me all the answers I needed. I countered that at this cancer center, I'd be practicing all that stuff, plus helping others—doing all the things he had taught me. But he refused to hear it.

I couldn't understand. Every time I sought healing, it was in service to my dad's lessons. I tried to explain, but he wouldn't listen. I was his creation, his ultimate art piece. If I left to learn at the feet of another, what colors would change? What textures?

I didn't understand the lesson but looked at my hands in my lap and thought it was all I could do, all I knew to do—*try*. Try like Hell to make something beautiful with the short amount of time we are given.

⁙

For over a month, I'd been thinking, *He better call me.*
And Preston was thinking, *She better call me.*
John would say, *Just call your Dad.* I'd cross my arms, point at that line
in the sand, and refuse. I needed my father to call me and say, *I'm sorry,
Robin.* I needed him to do that.

Around then, my heart developed a minor arrhythmia—sleepy beats
with seconds between followed by a rabbit thumping in my chest. I found a
doctor who fitted me with a monitor I wore as a halter beneath my T-shirt,
snug against the skin, holding me in. An assurance against floating away.
One evening, about a month into my father and I not speaking, I walked
to the oak behind the bunker where John and I still lived and knelt at its
trunk, closed my eyes to the sky, and pressed my hand to the heart monitor at my breast as though it were a walkie-talkie. I imagined my father
holding the other handset.

Sending out signals, hoping Dad's heart would respond, praying that
the electrical muscle within his chest would beat just one bit closer to
calling me, to reaching out across this rift abyss. I didn't wanna be the
first to cave. Stubborn of gut but soft of heart—I knew this wasn't the way.

Sight blurred by tears, eyes turned heavenward, I challenged God to
show me.

If you really love me and you're really there, I said aloud to nature, *I
need to see.*

It was a child's wish from my inner child's wounded heart. But it was
filled with childlike hope, which is perhaps the strongest, purest force in
the universe. Years later, I clearly see that it wasn't God's love I was seeking
evidence of.

⁙

Desiring direct proof from God has always been a tricky business.

The Levite priests who'd influenced the hem of my father's jeans had many
holy tasks, including carrying the Ark of the Covenant, which held the tablets

engraved with the Ten Commandments. The Ark itself was made from acacia wood, a cousin of the mesquite. It was draped in many veils of animal skins and bright blue fabric to conceal what was within. People said that the Ark was the seat of God—just looking at it would result in sudden death.

People risked their lives for just one glimpse. For some assurance in a random world filled with pain and injustice. Our hearts are too scarred and scared to return to the pure place of faith and hope that graces each of us as children before we see the sacred as separate—as a man in the sky, as tablets in a beautiful box, as our parents themselves.

When not two seconds after my asking for proof the biggest shooting star slashed the dark sky, I stood right up and walked into the bunker like I'd received marching orders. I called my father, and he answered. The first thing I said, because it was awkward, was, *You're not gonna believe this.* And I told him about the star.

And my dad said, *Of course, God loves you. You should never have to ask that.*

The prayer-worn patch of mud beneath the old oak. Humphrey slumped snuggly at my feet. The air that I breathed and the skin that felt its breeze. Preston's voice on the other end of the line. *This* was all the testimony I needed.

All I could say then was, *I miss you, Dad.*

And all he could say was, *I miss you too.*

I asked Preston if John and I could take him to lunch the next day. And he said, *I would love that. I would really love that.* And then he said, *I'm feeling very weary, so I'm gonna go lay down.*

I'd never heard my father say such a thing before: weary.

So I told him I loved him, and he said he loved me too. I told him I would see him tomorrow morning. And that was it.

John and I pulled up to Preston's house at 11:00 sharp that next morning. I was giddy—I had so much to tell my father. We'd sit down and apologize to each other like when we'd met on the San Antonio River and eat some Tex-Mex on a patio while Dad smoked. We'd laugh and listen and make plans, and never waste that kind of time again. We'd get back to good, for good this time.

I just wanted to run to my father with open arms, and I did. And found him lying there lifeless.

∴

Sometimes, it takes a while to get used to being a human being. Some people are never able to really make it. The boundary of the skin is too confining for the soul. All the little reminders they give themselves to stay here aren't enough.

The edge keeps meandering further and further.

We are born so raw, and I think part of us always needs to stay that way. Receptive and connected. What we hide is what we share. Sitting together in our unravel, we suffer a thousand apocalypses—a word itself which means, in Greek, "to reveal."

We're each imperfect, with a tendency toward tattering.

We are only as strong as we are vulnerable.

Unfinished hems are wearable hymns to remind us though our skin ends where another's begins, we're all just walking each other home, as Ram Dass said. Each raw hem is a threshold, whipping around like a riverbed, describing how you flow within.

With each step, there's that anchoring little ache that whispers and reveals:

The frays make us.

Chapter 14

HANDS

ANYTHING THAT MATTERED TWO SECONDS EARLIER MEANT nothing anymore. Everything spun, silent, and came to a point of queasy clarity.

All I could see were my father's eyes, sky-blue wide open. Staring at the ceiling, staring, staring. John tried to close them, but they kept popping back open, as though he'd seen something so beautiful that he couldn't look away, even in death. I was drawn to those blue pools as I had been from the start. Seasick, they were my horizon. I hovered over my father's face, placing myself in his gaze. His eyes were still so vivid, unbelievably bright as the day I first looked into them and saw myself reflected.

There's something inside, deep inside, that shines through the eyes. It's the thing that doesn't die, that was seeing me. That recognized me. I'd always attributed it to the flesh, that quality of vision—that it was somehow *in* those blue eyes. But there were his perfect eyes intact, just like they were when he was alive. Exactly the same. But he couldn't see me anymore.

We found out later that, in one single moment, my father's heart had just exploded.

∴

I tore myself from Dad's stare and looked around the room. Each glance was a photograph: his Star Wars bed sheets and technicolor Peter Max pillowcase. Sketchbook journals stacked neatly on his nightstand, topped with his most recent read, a book about Druids. He wore denim cut-off painting shorts, smudged with still-wet paint. His old holy-hemmed Levis lay next to him, waiting to be worn. His purple wizard T-shirt hanging on the closet door. Bright bursts of red glitter dotted his hands, bits of his process—his portrait of Selena Quintanilla propped unfinished in his studio area.

The moment was a macabre snow globe. The worst moment. Surreal. Unreal. Enraging. The sheer injustice of getting so close to something so true and clear and pure and having it stolen away from you was a sword in my gut.

John had covered Preston's body with a bright color-blocked afghan, hand-crocheted by my Grandmother Brown, and I curled up under it next to Dad. He was still somewhat warm, and I wrapped myself around him like I'd clung to him on the back of our Triumph. I wanted to fall asleep next to my father and have this all be a very bad dream. I lay there crying and praying, crying and praying.

And begging:

God. Just take me from this earth right now. I'm not far behind him. I'll find him and catch up to him in Brigadoon. I just know I can. Then I can tell him I love him and I'm sorry, and let's go on this next adventure together.

My heart galloped into a radical rhythm. For a second, it felt like I was gonna have a heart attack, and the thought brought me hope instead of panic. I smashed the hard plastic heart monitor against my sternum. It felt like a weight I just wanted to rip off. An anchor. Who fucking cared what my heart sounded like anymore—Its erratic beat was now the labored scrape of a ball and chain. My stubborn lungs kept on. Great swallows of breath became fuel for a fire within. When my pleas didn't work, I tried rage. Railing against God. *Fuck you for not taking me, too. For not letting him live just one day longer. One hour. Would that have been too much to ask?*

God could have their proof.

I wanted my father.

Half my arms were gone, half my legs. Half my heart. There was so much I'd needed to say, so much we were going to do. Preston's eyes stared into eternal wonder as my hot tears fell onto his face. I heard John say that people were arriving at the house—beloved neighbors, friends, officials. My mother.

The precious seconds left for me to be in contact with my father in his physical form were dwindling. No description of minutes, no rhythm of heart or portion of water could relate. Only my father's blue eyes and his glittery hands made any sense at all.

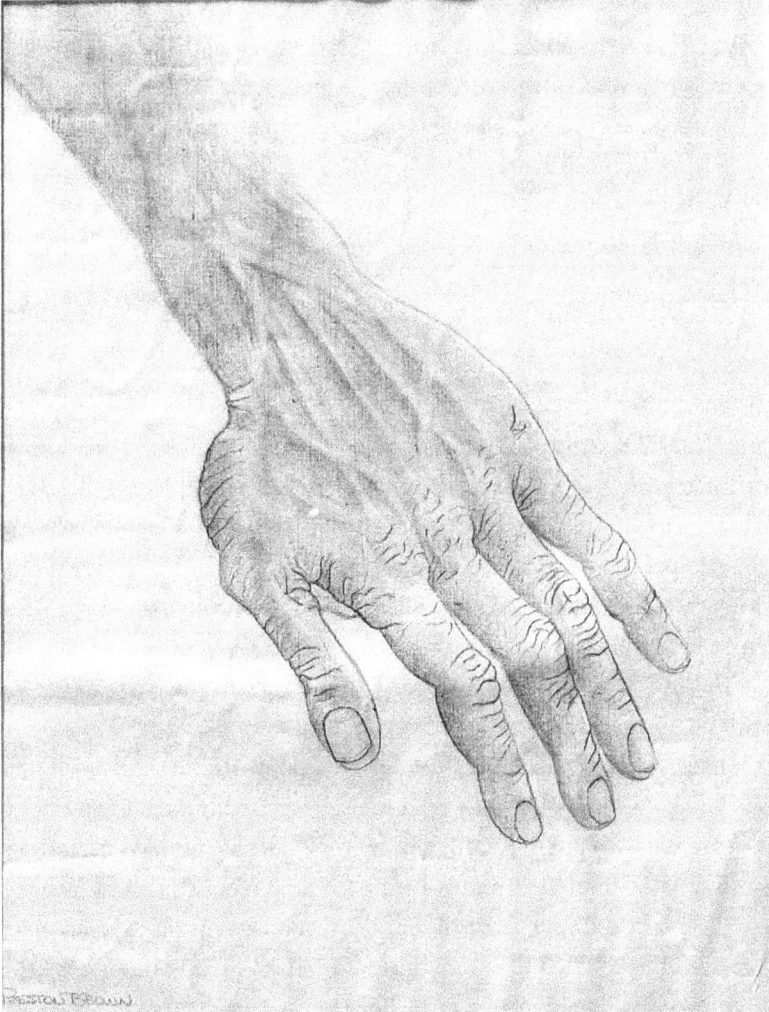

By Preston

As I held my father's hand for the last time, I studied it. Etched it into my mind. The weight and texture. The lines and paint smudges. The slick pink burn-wrought scars. The calluses and yellowed fingertips. The large flecks of glitter like an infrared sky. Hands of an artist, a sculptor, a smoker, a gardener. A sage. A father.

I thought of all the spiritual teachers my father had quoted over the years—their sayings about not being attached to the flesh. I had felt the warmth dissipate from my father's body and go where? His cold hand in mine I could hold for only moments more. None of us asked for this, but we're here now. Can't we honor how much we need each other? How precious we are to each other and how little time we have to share it?

From that night in the open-roof rock house, Preston's voice echoed in my head. From all the times he spoke it before. How he had been preparing me. How he had feared for my loneliness. And I had never understood what he meant.

∴

John had called Anna, and she had appeared faster than she'd ever shown up for anything. Someone had given her a ride, wheelchair and all. I don't remember what we said to each other; perhaps we didn't speak. If she hadn't shown up, I don't think I could've ever let go of his hand. Not for the first time was her presence painful; but for the very first time, it was merciful. I gave her time alone with him and wandered through my father's house.

Preston had always been very tidy from years in the Navy and years with his mother. But on this date, his house was immaculate. Every ashtray was empty and wiped clean. There wasn't a single stray crumb or cat hair anywhere. His books were all perfectly stacked. Aside from the outfit he was preparing to put on, all his clothes were hung and folded neatly. His trash can was empty and clean—he hadn't even replaced the trash bag.

He had no coffee; he'd run out of all his supplements. He had no toilet paper. I opened his fridge, sure to see the gallon of milk he always kept. But the only thing in there was the light bulb.

It was as if he'd known and prepared.

I stared into the cold, bright emptiness of the refrigerator as though it was the void itself until the sound of my mother's sobbing brought me back. I'd never heard her cry so quietly and authentically. I shuffled to the furniture partition that served as my father's doorway and saw that Anna had peeled away the afghan to reveal Preston's feet. She held his heels in her palms, her head on his soles, drenching them with tears.

I had seen my mom in all extremes, but I'd never seen her that sad in all the days of my life. Wheeling her back was like transporting a tranquilized tiger. Ever careful, in awe. She looked up at me with wet, makeup-smudged eyes and said she was ready to go now, too. Just let God take her.

This one time, we were on the same page.

∴

A crowd had formed on Dad's street with the silenced bright blue-and-red beacon of the ambulance. The neighborhood children and the men from the halfway house sat in the alleyway crying, arms around each other.

I went back inside as the paramedics gently loaded my father's body onto the stretcher. Someone handed me Dad's wallet—one of those canvas Velcro ones little kids carry, with a bright yellow Batman logo. Covered in paint smudges. Four dollars folded neatly inside, the exact price of a broken heart. I heard the sound of wheels again, smooth and clinical, this time carting away my soul, my human. Draped in a blue blanket like the Ark of the Covenant.

I couldn't peel my eyes from the sight, followed it until it was a tiny blue dot in my vision like the earth from space—all we know and love contained in a single speck. Still, my heart kept beating. I wasn't struck dead but stuck alive.

I gathered the sketch pads from Preston's nightstand, a few paint-brushes, his belt, and his Bible, and I walked out. I never went back. I didn't want anything. I just wanted him.

Outside, I told all the children, *The one thing Mr. Preston would want more than anything in this life is for all of you to keep painting. Every day. All of you. That's what would make him the happiest.*

With the proof of my father stacked in my lap, I sat still in John's truck as he spoke with people in the crowd. I stared with my own blue eyes at the flecks of red glitter that coated my fingers from holding my father's hands.

The light that had been on him was now on me.

∴

There were so many times my father and I couldn't speak about so many things.

We didn't have the language. Alike in our loneliness, we shared time for a little while on this planet and held hands.

An overwhelming love for Earth often strikes astronauts in orbit. Upon return, they struggle with what vocabulary could fully express just how much we're all each other has. Looking back over our lives and looking forward to the future—both of these things happen right now, with what we can feel with our hands, what we can touch, and how we might shape and be shaped by it. The warmth is here and now.

As much as my father dreamed about the cosmos and drew stars on everything, he was more interested in the ordinary miracles of tending to what was in proximity to him—what was at hand. Dad's lessons may have centered on feet, and I was drawn to the wonder in his eyes, but really, it's the hands—all of our hands—that love.

Any positive changes we want to make in this world start at our fingertips. I try to honor this wisdom in my clothing through symbol and skill. When something has been lovingly held, that feeling resonates—the warmth of one tender moment extending out, infinite.

Maybe it's no accident that the parts of the clock that tick away time are called hands.

Chapter 15

REVERSIBLE

THE DAY RIGHT AFTER MY FATHER DIED, I HAD AN APPOINTMENT
with the cardiologist to remove my heart monitor. Those little straps tight
around my solar plexus felt like the only things holding my chest together. I
wondered what would happen when they removed it—would I float away?
Crumple to the floor? I'd probably burst open and flood the place.

Instead, once they removed the harness, I just sat there, somehow still
contained. I waited in the cold, bright doctor's office for an eternity, it
seemed—all quiet but for machine hums and hushed voices outside the
door. My hiccupping heartbeat within, clumsy and dogged and pissing
me off with its tenacity. The sheer nerve of it. I was hopeful the doctor
would come in and confirm all my suspicions: at any moment, my heart,
too, was going to explode.

So, when she sat before me with a look of concern, I wasn't fazed. She
had questions about my results. The pattern of my heart's workings on
the printout before her was erratic and unreadable. Perhaps the monitor
had stopped working?

I managed to tell her that I'd found my father dead the day before, of
all that had happened, and how hard I prayed. This woman removed her
glasses and rubbed her eyes.

In all the years I've been doing this, she said, *I've never seen the moment a heart breaks.* The exact electricity, the precise, decisive moment—it was something she'd never captured. I don't remember if she showed me the results—what constellations the beats formed, what peaks and flat planes, what waves. Whatever was revealed was plain to me already; no proof was necessary.

∴

In the weeks after, I became my own heart. If that stubborn fucker wouldn't stop, then neither could I.

I must've made a thousand cookies and cakes back at the retirement center. Still in transition, so many mouths to feed and doses to administer, diapers to change, and dishes to wash. The beat of routine and the care of the needs of others tethered me enough, at least. Still, the tsunami inside kept crashing nonetheless, gravity pulling tears steady and silent from my eyes. Never before or since have I dug so deeply into my clown bag, relying on the lessons I'd learned at the stilted striped feet of High Pockets.

The show must go on.

It was lockstep with what Preston had mentioned obsessively over our last year together—how I was to carry on the work. Through art and helping others, I was to fulfill our purpose. To finish what we had started.

But first, I had to finish his painting.

∴

It was just like Preston to leave with everything in perfect order except the completion of the painting. But then, I knew. I knew he expected me to finish it: a life-size canvas portrait of Selena Quintanilla surrounded by roses, with her beautiful name in glittery script at the bottom. It was meant to be a gift to the Sonora family, owners of Dad's favorite San Antonio Tex-Mex restaurant called El Milagrito. It was where we were meant to meet the day he died.

Years before, I'd helped Dad with a mural of Emiliano Zapata that once graced the side of the restaurant. Over endless cups of coffee and plates of chalupas, the owners and staff had fed and sat with my father for years. It was his surrogate home.

Portrait of Emiliano Zapata by me & Dad, El Milagrito

We decided that El Milagrito would be the perfect setting for my father's send-off, and before the date of the memorial, I presented the painting to the Sonoras. There'd only been a little left to do, anyway, and I tended to it the best I could. But when I gave it to Mrs. Sonora, she insisted it wasn't finished.

I need you to sign his signature, she told me.

I said I couldn't do it.

But you're the only one who can, she insisted.

In cursive, I scribbled out Preston's signature, his first name and our last, followed by the year. I had forged my parents' signatures so many times over the years for school shit, but this was the first time it felt wrong.

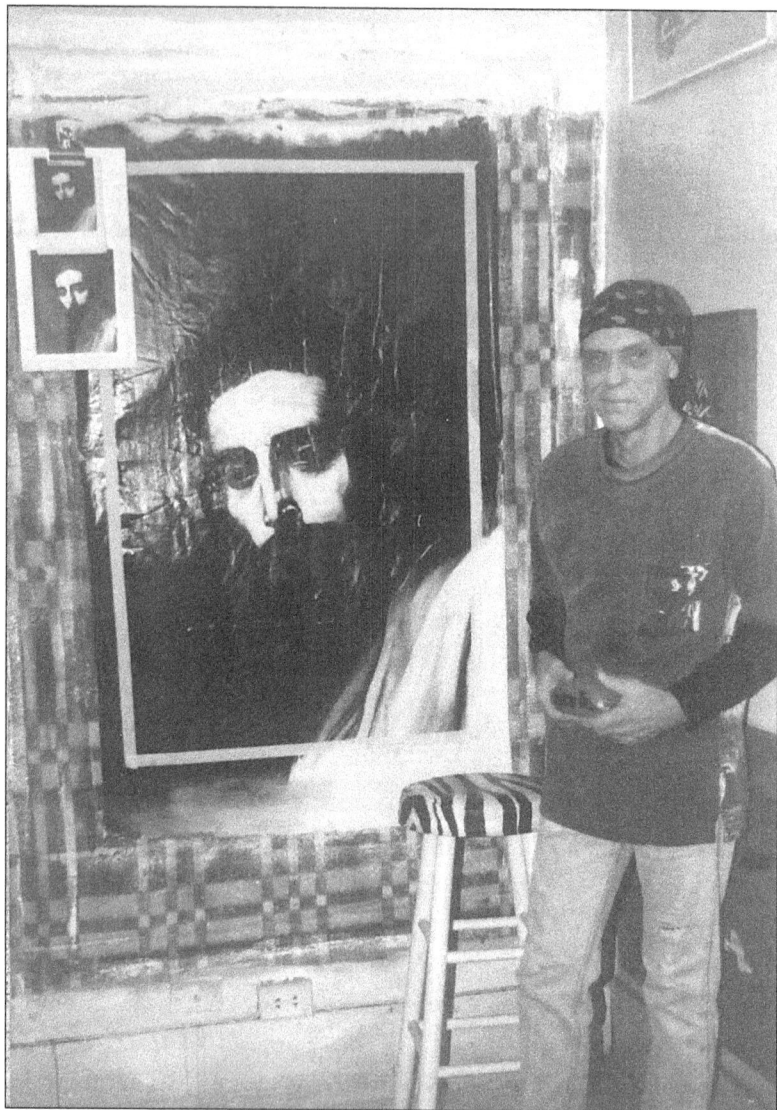

∴

Preston's particular method of grieving was always to paint through it. He cried, of course, but painting was the thing. It wasn't about transforming his pain into beauty but continuing to insist upon beauty, even from within the deepest pain. In a way, Dad lived in a perpetual state of grief. Most of his works were of people who had long passed, whose legacies never left my father for a moment. His subjects had given their life to spirit and left this earth amid turmoil. He painted them so they wouldn't disappear.

Dad didn't care much what happened to the canvases themselves once they were finished. They could be destroyed like those Zen sand paintings, and he wouldn't have batted an eye. It was, again, for him, about the process and not the product. He created portraits of Rembrandt over and over and over.

Not so much because he was so moved by Rembrandt's art but by his humanity. He never showed those particular works to anyone besides me, and when he was done with them, he'd give them away, paint over them, or trash 'em.

Instead of being a glimpse into his soul, each of my father's paintings was like a little mirror, reflecting our shared mortality. *Do what you will with me*, they seemed to say, *but look at this person and remember*.

Remember.

Bob Marley, by Preston

∴

Dad was remembered well in a perfectly small neighborhood ceremony at El Milagrito. The golden-toothed matriarch of the Sonora family came out of retirement to tie on her thin cotton apron and prepare refried beans and Spanish rice, shared by neighborhood poets and parents, addicts and artists, amid readings, songs, jokes, tears, and laughter. Tex-Mex sacraments taken in memory and communion celebrated under the watchful gaze of Selena's portrait. It was a beautiful day. I've forgotten a lot of the details, but I remember the warmth.

And then it's over—the holy sacraments turn back into crackers and grape juice and you're expected to get on with it, immediately. That's when the real grief sets in. The kind that's hard to witness, that we don't know how to talk about.

My father had advised me that, when he was gone, he wanted me not to cry. He, who bore witness through painting his grief, could not see himself as the subject. By his own account, Preston hadn't feared the process of *dying*, but of *leaving*. He didn't want his passing to be a burden on anyone. That's why he hadn't shared with me any inklings he might've had about his impending death, why he didn't wanna come to me for help with groceries. He couldn't fully reveal his weariness because he felt he'd be a hardship. So, instead, he kept it all so tight in his heart that the thing just exploded.

None of us are exempt from death, but also, none of us are exempt from life. If we wanna love, we're gonna lose; there's no two ways about it—the holy both.

I felt so fucking alone in my grief after the memorial. I worked and worked. John and I did end up moving to Bandera. Everything on the outside ticked on as though the world hadn't ended. But there was no one to sit with in my grief. John was my shoulder to cry on, but he was busy. Anna mourned, but she was so checked out on pain meds there was no getting through. Amy was equally absent in her addictions, and Thovas was devastated to the core, but angry and apart.

I needed my dad to help me process the death of my dad.

∴

I looked for him everywhere, and searched for him every way I could—eyes peeled for signs, seeking a symbolic conversation. Dad had always said he wanted to return as a turkey buzzard after he died so he could soar over the Texas Hill Country. I suppose each vulture is a wizard alchemist, turning death into renewal. I'd watch those great black birds kettling in the blue Texas sky every day, but mostly I saw 'em huddled around deer carcasses on the side of the road on our long, frequent drives between Bandera and Pleasanton. It just felt cold and grotesque. The otherworldly things that always happened with my father were done and gone. How was I to find magic on this earth anymore?

As a kid, I often sat and cried in frustration because I wasn't as smart as my father. I so desperately wanted to communicate with him on his level. I beat myself up for my learning disabilities. I'd always compare myself to him, and I'd always fall short.

At thirty-three, I sat with my father's journals on my lap, turning each priceless page. Of all the swollen sketchbooks he'd filled over his life, only these two were left. All the others he had chunked in the trash over the years. Not that I'd ever really understood them—each page filled with his neat handwriting in black ink quotes from artists and mystics, metaphysical wonderings and manifestos, research on ancient civilizations.

He was so earnest and anxious to learn everything in the world there is to know. My father would read a thick book in twenty-four hours and then be able to tell you everything in it. His notes in the margins like runes. Every highlighter he ever owned was worn to the nub.

Preston was searching, searching, searching, always and trying to see how it's all connected. And I followed his feet, seeking myself by reading *him*. Now that his light was gone, I had to create my own.

∴

It was one of those sweet spring days in Central Texas, when the rains have been gentle and summer hasn't walloped yet, that we poured my father's ashes into the Medina. It wasn't anything formal—just me and John and Thovas. The three of us listening to all Preston's favorites, especially The Waterboys and the song "Our Town" by Iris Dement. Dad and I listened to that song nonstop in the months before we fought, before he passed. It was our anthem at the time, a hymn to the hometown we dreamt of.

The dense gray remains of my father seeped into the Medina's clear waters, swirling on the surface before being absorbed. He poured from my hands that held tight to the generic cardboard box from the funeral home, laminated to look like wood. It was quiet and so quick, the colossus of my life reduced to clay and reunited with the waters.

The cottonwood trees that line the Medina River that we stood among that day had known my father since he was a baby. They'd raised him, cradled him, and watched him learn to swim. A few days after Preston passed, the oldest of them all collapsed into the river and washed downstream. There was a gaping hole where its once towering trunk stood for a century. The landscape was entirely changed.

The lore of the cottonwood tree is that she gave birth to the stars. Truly, star-shaped buds emerge in early spring from their branches and then, later in the season, burst in puffs of shimmery cotton as seeds. In winter, if you break off a cottonwood branch, the design of a five-pointed star is revealed within.

As mapmakers had once consulted the stars, I began to map my inner terrain by those cottonwoods. There was the Medina River, and there was everywhere else.

∴

I still had a bone to pick with God. I'd prayed and prayed that Dad and I could move to Bandera together. And now we had, only one of us wasn't alive. Had I not been specific enough? Was this some big joke? I wanted to communicate with my dad *himself,* not through some medium whom I couldn't see or touch, and who seemed to have a messed-up sense of humor.

So I wrote my father letters every day for who knows how long. I'd scribble out something for Preston, stuff it into an envelope with "Dad" scrawled on the outside, walk down to this one cottonwood on the river and tuck it amid the roots, or nail it right to the trunk.

That tree probably had a thousand letters on it. Sometimes, I'd show up, and several would be missing, gone with the current. I always hoped Dad was receiving them somehow and that he would know. He would receive my words and know I was so sorry and I missed him and I loved him with my whole broken heart. That he was the most human, the best human. That he had taught me so much.

I wanted to lay these words at the foot of the tree so I could rise and walk from there feeling lighter, somehow, "better." It didn't matter how many letters I wrote, though. I still just felt alone. I couldn't sense my father and couldn't make sense of God.

∴

When a baby's in the womb, it has no fucking clue that just the teeniest space separates it from the outside world—that hovering beyond the thinnest boundary of fluid and skin are sights and sounds and souls entirely unimaginable. Maybe beneath the water's surface, I could finally hear my father. It was worth a try.

Each river is a threshold, a line separating two territories—the seen and unseen, known and unknown, before and after, life and death. Solid ground is uncertain. Within the river, there's only depth. Immersing myself in the center of the Medina was the center point of my journey. Every step I had taken through Fire and Ice had led me there. And every step I would take after that was to flow from it.

I felt the weight of pain like an anchor. So much I couldn't let go of pulling me down like rocks in my pocket: the homecoming I had anticipated for Dad and me, the conversation we never got to have. I wanted to hear an answer, but beneath the water, I could only hear my heart. I'd been looking for signs of my father, of God, everywhere—the sky, the ground, the landscape. But the *true* homecoming was to my own heart. The conversation I mourned was always meant to be an internal one.

Being brave doesn't mean not crying or acting tough. It means sinking into your heart, which is doing its best all the time to keep you existing. It doesn't matter where you go or who or what you're surrounded by; you are never for a moment separate from love or God. The breath in my chest was dwindling, and my heart was near to bursting. At a point, the hero of any journey must become their own guide. I wasn't sure I could do it alone, but it wasn't up to me. Sinking deeper, my feet grazed the riverbed, which felt to all the world like my father's hands, urging breath back into my lungs.

∴

Sometimes, people emerge from baptisms or rituals with the hope that from then on, all their grief and anxiety and suffering will be gone. *POOF!* Like magic. I wanted that to be true more than anything, that whatever had happened in those waters would fix everything forever.

I crawled back onto the banks of the Medina that afternoon alone, wrapped myself in a towel, and watched the sky's gentle transition from blue to golden scarlet to ink black. I hadn't emerged onto some dreamy opposite shore where all my pain had been magically whisked away. The cottonwood connecting heaven and earth still stood next to me, my letters to Preston nailed to its trunk, grown soggy with rain and dew, giving themselves to the river. More than a permanent remedy, feeling the divine within us is a perpetual reminder.

Our body is born once, but our heart is born many times.

That day marked a sea change. The wheel of my life that'd been cranking one way slowed. Like a child twirling in a skirt then stopping, each ripple of cloth cocooning. Torque's lift and lurch, upward and inward, then spinning back the other direction.

I would never be without grief. It became part of my fabric. And if I knew anything, it was how to work with fabric.

∴

Each piece of fabric has two sides—what the world sees and what lies against your skin. In a way, I think the hidden parts should be more beautiful. It sends a message, ya know? Beauty for beauty's sake is knowing that no one might ever notice.

It's purely loving how things are made.

The "face" of the fabric, the "right" side—we can get so stuck thinking life has to look one way, that love, or healing, or creativity, or grieving has to look one way. None of these things happen in the past or some imagined future, but in the present. Miracles are a counterforce; each moment is an opportunity to turn everything around.

What do you spin with the light you are given?

Releasing is in the telling, even as it is unfolding. In the middle of a miracle, God's art exhibit we're blessed to exist in. Once we look past ourselves and on to the possibilities of our contributions, we no longer have time or the hunger for such validation. Stay bewildered and in love with your possibilities. Thank your ego for your survival, and then politely set it free. Jump into your spirit that lives in your soul, get busy creating beauty and love, and stay so intoxicated with heart songs that you never remember to wonder about the mediocrity of life again.

Those who have not swum
through the oceans of grief
have never touched the floor
of their own being
where they find the sands
of understanding
that allows the commonplace
to become extraordinary.
Grief is a place
where one drowns
until they're awake.

Chapter 16

RED HEARTS

ALL MY LIFE, WHEN I'D LOOK AT MATERIAL SOMEONE ELSE neglected or didn't want, I'd feel the soul in it by touching it, holding it, and envisioning all the potential of what could be. Silks, denim, cotton, or even color can shift into something else. Everything can evolve and inspire awe, but it's got to begin in the heart. Because when you use your heart, you can create anything from what initially seems like nothing.

My father had taught me so much, and he had made beautiful art, but my mother was the person who really lived that lesson. Anna had shown me how to see pieces of material, get to know them, and put them together. It was something never really spoken, and it was also something that never, *ever*, stopped.

I'd always wondered when it all began for her, that process. I knew so very little of her childhood outside of the truly horrific.

It was around 1990, about seven years before my father passed when we finally learned the answer.

∴

That year, I was mid-spiral at the retirement center. I hadn't yet found Humphrey; I hadn't yet visited Hippocrates. On a rare and random visit to Mom, I found her shrunken to about half her typical body weight. Anna was in her early fifties then, still drinking, and God knows what else. She didn't look or seem well at all, and it was safe to assume she'd contracted AIDS. Fearing the worst, she got a test, which showed that she was, instead, severely diabetic. Her pancreas was sputtering.

She had to quit drinking for real, and she did. And then she went ahead and blew everyone's mind by seeing a psychiatrist. Mom's history with psychiatry was pretty bleak, man. Electroshock therapy, straightjackets, and pills that never quite clicked would be enough to scare anyone away, but Anna was one of the bravest people I ever met.

The psychiatrist diagnosed her with a lot of stuff we kinda knew and expected: bipolar disorder, borderline personality disorder, manic/depressive disorder, PTSD, anxiety, depression. But there was one more that wasn't as familiar: dissociative identity disorder (DID, what they used to call multiple personality disorder).

∴

I'd always believed that the gashes to Anna's psyche from her childhood had entirely fractured her mind, even before we learned the diagnosis. Imagining something or someone being "shattered" or "broken" is effective—but it's completely wrong. It's just how that person's beautiful brain is wired for survival. The alters are there, more or less, until the end, always protecting the individual. Sometimes the way they go about this is paradoxical—safety isn't easily defined. Even angels can appear terrifying.

The doctor discovered my mother's alters through hypnosis. I don't recall all their names and all their functions. There was a child-like one, and one named Iris, who seemed to have it out for me, specifically. Discerning the alters' personalities and behaviors from what was distinctly Mom's was never really something we tried to do. It was just a relief to have a name for all the whip-fast changes Anna went through. Learning that secrecy and denial are part of the program with DID helped us reconcile a little of what had gone on throughout our lives. People with DID are rarely violent; usually, these people are more apt to end up on the receiving end of abuse, which was undoubtedly true for Mom. Her condition isn't why she was so abusive—the abuse she suffered is why she was so abusive.

Everything else going on with Anna could be somewhat addressed with medication, which she was surprisingly down with. Better psych meds were finally rolling out. Because of her alcoholism, Mom had never taken any kind of medication consistently. Now that she was sober, she gave it all she had.

And we got one glorious year.

∴

"Normal" is such a bad word in so many ways, but after decades of "beyond fucked-up," our family welcomed normal with open arms. We didn't talk about the past or clear the air, but it felt nice enough to sit together and get to know each other all over again. Mom, Thovas, and I formed a little triad. Every opportunity I got, I was over there with them, having coffee and laughing. We'd shared those moments before, but they were fleeting and spaced out from each other like jet lag leap years.

Mom and I spent hours discussing art, AA, angels and saints, God, and textiles. We'd eat enchiladas at El Milagrito and cross the street to the Catholic church to pray the rosary. Then we'd hit all the thrift stores on the South Side and stock up on worn flannel shirts, Mexican dresses, and Ziploc bags stuffed with lace and trimmings. Back at her house, we'd work together on this little clothing collection Mom had been putting together for a while. I'd pay her to make a piece for me when I could.

I wasn't a designer in those moments. I was just a daughter.

We flowed in a way we never had before. All the bits of debris that had been dammed up were finally released, and I felt free enough to jump into the stream alongside my mother—help direct how these scraps might reassemble. Month after month, I couldn't believe the gift.

∴

In the end, it wasn't alcohol that ended that string of good days, but candy.

Anna lived in a government high-rise building for the aging and ailing, which was located right across the street from a Walgreens. Whenever she got her SSI check, she'd sneak over to the store—sometimes in the middle of the night—and stock up on Moon Pies and those jelly orange slices with the sugar all over. Then she'd roll out to the curb right in front of the store and eat every sugary bit.

Mom got so deathly ill from all the sugar that she'd have to take more and more insulin. Her bones deteriorated so severely from osteoarthritis that merely bumping into her caused 'em to crumble. A string of back surgeries began, which ended with her losing the use of her legs. She relied on a wheelchair and a daily dose of enough prescription opiates to knock out a whole circus full of elephants. She gained a large amount of weight and her limbs lost circulation. She got emphysema and a complete set of dentures.

Ray doted on Anna hand and foot all he could. His sole possession was a little deep fryer he set up in Mom's kitchen, with which he cooked every meal.

When Ray got his check from the VA, he'd leave for a while to sleep under the Nolan Street bridge by the McAllister freeway with his buddies, sprawled out on mattresses under the stars and crisscrossing cement. Anna'd call me crying to go find him, and I'd drive out there and sit among these houseless folk, most of whom were veterans. They sat cradling little Styrofoam bowls of baked beans from the Salvation Army, telling stories like you've never heard about life and loss and despair and gratitude. Ray told everyone I was his daughter come to scoop him; then he'd put a few little shards of treasures in his pocket for my mother, and I'd drive him back home. Before I left, I filled their fridge with diet sodas and made sure they had all they needed in the way of candy and fry-cook sundries.

Because fuck it.

Anna and Ray, A.R.T.

At that point, it was the most logical and gentle philosophy. Release, and allow. Nothing was gonna change. We'd had our good year with her, and, in a crazy way, Anna was happy. Maybe it was all the prescription drugs, or Ray, or the bags and bags of orange-slice gummies. Sure, she'd get pissed about being stuck in her chair. She missed driving, and she missed drinking.

But Anna was OK if—every single day—she could create *something*.

.•.

Mom's wings were clipped, but she refused to be caged. San Pedro Park became her territory for found objects. She'd fill her chair's Naugahyde saddlebags with bits of birds' nests and feathers, acorns, leaves, and shiny candy wrappers. Everything else she needed came from Walgreens.

After Valentine's Day, Mom wheeled over and dug all the discarded hearts from the trash—stacked as many as she could on her lap and brought 'em back home. She lined the hearts' interiors with old fabric and, with a caulk gun, she applied all her park finds to their glittery faces. Oatmeal canisters were another preferred canvas she transformed into fanciful handbags for a fairy tale ball.

As the circumference of Mom's territory shrunk, her drive to create grew increasingly urgent. Anything and everything within her reach became material and then ethereal.

.•.

A few months before he passed, Preston and I visited Anna.

We huddled in Mom's tiny home, hazy with cigarette smoke and deep-fried air. Mom, in her wheelchair, sat surrounded by little snippets of material from the wooden to the woven, scintillating and lacy and jagged and every texture in between. She was a bowerbird, a living mosaic, a queen on her throne in the land of the discarded but not forgotten.

Dad picked up and put down each piece in a rhythmic ritual. They were both soaring in their element, and I was amazed. I could only sit back and watch these two humans—who had made me—make magic. But my parents weren't artists because they made art. They were artists because they were alive: the way they sipped their coffee, the way they squinted through the smoke to look out the window, the way they inhaled. They couldn't help it, and despite everything, couldn't help seeing it in each other.

My mother's mind survived by the virtue of creativity, and my father's mind refused to unlearn the art that held his lonely childhood together. As low as they could each go—and Lord knows they got low—they could go equally as high. Drugs had nothing to do with the equation. A stubborn insistence on creativity above all else, in the face of all else, allowed them to survive. Hell, sometimes thrive.

We think we need so much to be happy, but all we really need is within reach, as long as we have someone to share it with. Someone who doesn't judge or begrudge us our creation. Someone who sees the same way as us. Who sees *us*.

Just as we were leaving, Dad told Anna she was one of the most fantastic and gifted artists he'd ever seen or known in this life. And I mean, I've never seen my mother smile from ear to ear in all my years. Preston was always very careful about the words he chose to speak. His journals overflowed with thoughts bubbling over, but his speech he edited like an X-Acto knife collage. His compliment to Anna was no little thing.

In the car, I asked Dad if he meant it. *One hundred percent*, he replied. *The art she's making*, he continued, *is borderline childlike and borderline genius. But she nails it. In a way that only she can.*

∴

To work with color is to work with light. We see color at all because white light is bent, reflected, and scattered. Because it's wounded. My parents lived in full color all the time, but to me, they were always blue and red. Preston, the blue—those eyes, those jeans. Anna, of course, red as fury, as blood.

The bit of paint-splattered denim that was my father, overlaid with the faded scarlet scrap of showgirl garb that was my mother, created the most beautiful garment I could ever dream up.

To be the blessed witness of their brilliant mending was to glimpse the thread of God. None of us knew at the time that my father's words were his parting gift to Anna on this Earth, but each of us knew, in that moment, that a wound had been dressed.

∴

The muses aren't the material but speak through the tools, sparking signals in a language of symbols we can only read backward. The wounds have been the way. Back to where we started, brought to our knees, eye level with those small oracles that speak directly to our hearts.

The hearts on my garments are beating blood-red Band-Aids over arrow wounds. They're a poultice for the pain that lies beneath and the promise of what might fill the gaping holes in our souls. The person who slung the most arrows of all is the one who showed me how to heal them.

The anatomical hearts on Anna's dolls, the sacred heart of Mary on her Virgen de Guadalupe creations—forever and always, no matter what, my mother insisted upon a heart upon it all. It was often the only way she knew how to communicate love. God, how she wanted to love so badly. She just couldn't figure out how.

Those hearts were all her holy selves coming together as a whole. Unbroken and urgent and bright as the sun's core. Love doesn't try to figure shit out or solve anything. It just shines. Radiant and boundless. Dangerous. Refined.

Chapter 17

RABBITS

AS A CHILD, AS MUCH AS I COULD HOLD ONTO OR KEEP TRACK of anything, I collected rabbits—porcelain figurines and those fur-footed keychains that I now find horrible. Once, Thovas and I found a fat furry bunny in the alleyway behind one of our various homes and begged and begged to keep it. We didn't get our wish but had a pretty great afternoon of bunny-cuddling.

Holidays always depressed Anna, but Easter was the one holiday she celebrated without fail every year. From the time we were small, she'd tell us the Easter Bunny was real and that she knew where he lived. It drove us crazy, and we pleaded with her to tell us where. She'd get a mischievous twinkle in her brown bunny eyes and tease us that someday she'd tell us, but not today.

And, oh man, her Easter baskets. Mom would find the funkiest old handwoven baskets at thrift stores, paint them, cover them with pictures of saints and glitter, and stash them full of candy (that she'd dip into, herself, of course). It was the one thing where she ever went all out for us kids. Throughout the years, anytime she appeared somewhat clear, Thovas and I knew we could ask her if today was the day she'd tell us where the Easter bunny lived. And again and again, *No, not today.*

•••

After Preston died, Anna's health flat-out deflated. It was a mix of heart-break and just overall decline; all her various ailments kept piling on like cards in a deck. She reached a point around the year 2000 where she couldn't function without around-the-clock care. By that time, John and I were pretty much free of the retirement center, and I found myself able to be my mother's caretaker, a role I slid back into like riding a bicycle.

We moved Mom out to Bandera to be near us, to a little nursing home about a block away from our house. John and I'd just moved into a bigger place, an old farmhouse that was falling down around us that we had started working on and fixing up.

Anna was pissed about the idea of a nursing home, but the staff agreed to let me decorate Mom's room however we wanted to make it more welcoming for her. Maybe they were expecting framed pictures of grand-children and embroidered pillows with sayings about golf and gardening, but of course, that wasn't what we had in mind. We painted Anna's room hot pink and hung pictures of the Virgen de Guadalupe. I stocked up on Diet Cokes, Moon Pies, Bluebell vanilla ice cream, and tall prayer can-dles from the Mexican grocery store. Clipped fresh roses went into old cut-crystal tumblers and carnival glass from the thrift store, all along the windowsill. It did the trick, and Mom gave in.

I stayed with her as much as I could, sitting with her and Ray, who'd stowed away. Anna's oxygen levels were depleting so quickly as the emphy-sema progressed that her mind floated in and out between this world and another. She saw things that weren't there that confused her. She got angry and frustrated with the staff. My mother was a terrible patient, throwing things and yelling. It reached the point where she tried to escape as soon as she saw an opportunity. She flung prayer candles against her windowpane until it shattered, then wheeled herself over and tried to pull herself out the window. Because of her size and the fact that she couldn't use her legs, it was a sad scene—she got stuck halfway through, shards of glass littering her hair and piercing her palms.

So, the nursing home kicked her out—just set Anna in her wheelchair on the sidewalk with her box of medicine and called me up. They wanted to admit her to a psych ward in a hospital, and they did, but that was also a disaster. She and Ray stayed with us for a few nights, but John was worried about Anna dying in our home—I'd never wanna step foot in it again if that were to happen. I couldn't wrap my brain around finding Mom another nursing home, plus she was banned forever for her behavior at the last one. All I knew was I'd never let her stay somewhere she would be kicked to the curb, never.

We were able to find a miraculous little cabin nearby, tiny but perfect. I set out to recreate the same atmosphere as before, like a little old house in Mexico—a holy day to live within, a celebration of life, even as it's ending. Especially then.

We arranged hospice, which included a medical bed, a bed for Ray, and a small cot for me. Because from the minute Anna moved in, I never left her side.

∴

I'd always had to love my mother from afar, even when we were right next to each other. In the two months Mom spent on hospice in that little cabin, I was able to get physically closer to her than I ever had in my life. I'd hold her long, elegant hands slowly turning blue from a lack of oxygen. Place my hands on her feet, which were blackening from gangrene. It was like she was decomposing while still alive. This woman who hadn't gone without makeup a day in her life, who'd shimmied for folks at the Pink Pussycat on stems that wouldn't quit, surrounded always by the scent of gardenia mixed with the plumes from her ever-present cigarette—now laid like an animated corpse, a macabre ragdoll rendition of Anna. But to me, she had never looked so beautiful.

Sometimes, her mind would come to, and she'd immediately wanna paint things. It was getting close to Halloween, so John and I brought her a variety of pumpkins to paint. She sat up in her chair with glitter and paints and just went to town on them. Every single pumpkin was decked out and set about her room among lit prayer candles and strung marigolds. It was like living inside a Día de los Muertos *ofrenda* Anna had hand-crafted for herself. But she didn't stop there.

As the days wore on, she began painting everything in sight: her coffee cup, her hands, the telephone. She put glitter on everything, everywhere. Big bottles of the stuff mingled with prescription vials and were almost as vital at that point. There was no way to keep it contained. Little scraps of light were strewn everywhere, smudged on medical equipment, in the sheets, in Mom's hair, and all over her suffocating hands.

Anna's last days, when she was conscious, were filled with this kind of exuberant creation. And laughter—Mom's gallows humor. Ray and John and I, often Thovas and sometimes Amy, huddled together in this bizarre scene of bedazzled decay, laughing down the hours, staring mortality in its jack-o-lantern face.

∴

At one point, Thovas and I had enough. We knew the end was near; the signs were everywhere. After all the shitty things that had happened to us at our mother's hands, we needed closure; we needed answers. We stood together at Anna's bedside and demanded to know where the Easter Bunny lived.

That look of mischief we knew all too well danced across Mom's brown eyes. *Gimme ten dollars, and I'll tell you*, she rasped. Thovas fished ten bucks from his wallet and handed it to her. She crumpled the bill and stuffed it under her butt in the bed, looking up at us cryptically.

No, she yawned, *not today*, and fell right back asleep.

∴

My mother hated closed doors. They reminded her too much of the time she spent locked in the attic as a child. She always needed an escape route. In the little cabin where she spent her last days, we kept the doors always open. October weather in Central Texas can be so gentle, sometimes. Loose leaves blew whispers in and out. There was no fear. There was only welcome.

When Mom felt well enough to sit in her chair, I'd wheel her to the front doorway as I busied myself in the kitchen—up to my elbows forever in vanilla ice cream for her bottomless milkshakes. Over the breeze and *Hank Williams' Greatest Hits*, I sometimes heard Mom talking.

Who are you talking to, Mom? I asked over my shoulder one day.

You didn't see him? she replied. *Well, he was standing right there talking to me. Your father.*

I walked over to her in a daze, my hands frozen.

Now he's out there in the yard, leaning on that tree and smoking a cigarette. Can't you see him? He's wearing his maroon and navy blue-striped shirt. She pointed. But all I could see was the wind.

What did he say? I managed.

He said he had come to get me. He's out there every day. But I told him I'm not ready yet. So he said just to let him know, and he'll keep checking in.

Then she waved a weak little *see-ya-later* toward the tree as if it were the most usual thing in the world. For the dying, they say, it is usual. Commonplace to have lost loved one's scraping around, waiting on you like they were waiting in line at the DMV. I'd always imagined that after we die, we turn into this incredible energy that bolts right into the sky, swimming and soaring and zooming all around the planets. Smoking a fucking cigarette and wearing a striped shirt, waiting around all lonely, and visiting your ex-wife wasn't my idea of what the afterlife looked like. It damn sure wasn't Brigadoon.

As much as Anna told me that Preston was completely fine and calm, I couldn't shake it. I was scared. So fucking afraid of the unknown and of what was happening to Mom. I felt so alone on this Earth, and what? After death, we're STILL alone?

The best way to dispel fear is to learn all you can and seek understanding about what you're avoiding. My father taught me we were put on this Earth to learn. All the knowledge poured into his sketchbooks reaffirmed that but didn't come to a solution. There was simply no way to outsmart it. The only way we learn how to live is by learning how to die.

∴

Time had become fluid; each moment a fleeting eternity. As Anna shed her masks one by one, she refused to keep even her oxygen mask on. Times when she would, it didn't matter. All that breath pumping full-blast—her body couldn't keep up.

One day, she fell into a deep sleep that Hank Williams and vanilla milkshakes couldn't rouse her from. Ray tried his best. John, too. Hospice came out and checked her vitals. She'd fallen into a coma and would likely be gone within a day or two. They said we could speak to her, and she could hear us. But she wouldn't speak again.

I sat with this information as I sat with Anna.

Was this my chance to tell her everything that was on my heart? To hold her and touch her? She, with no choice but to absorb it all? Mom had never been able to plug into anything sweet or kind anyone had ever said to her. Maybe she didn't feel like she deserved it, which is why seeing Preston's compliment to Anna really land had been so moving—I'd been telling her that same thing for years, only to be met with a side-eye-roll. She didn't trust anything positive, especially about herself. She shooed off everything good I ever said to her like an annoying gnat. Often, it earned me a slap.

This time, she was a captive audience, for once. I called my siblings to let them know it was time.

Thovas arrived immediately. Amid our quiet vigil, Anna's eyes popped open and searched the room. We huddled around her, cooing in low voices, *Hi Mama, we're here*. She wanted to sit up in bed, of all things, so John and Thovas hoisted her dwindling but sturdy frame. Propped her up all comfortable.

Mom's whole life, she had avoided eye contact with me. It made her squirm; she said she didn't want anyone staring into her soul. Out of habit, I glanced sidelong at her. I didn't wanna put her off, especially at that moment, but her eyes were clearer than I'd ever seen, Earth-solid, warm brown, and steady. She looked so alert, so beautiful. She looked present.

Unsure of how to handle this gift, Thovas and I trod lightly.

Mom? You have to tell us where the Easter Bunny lives.

Anna stared into the middle distance for a while. A warm smile crept over her as she beckoned us closer. My brother and I leaned in and held hands.

The Easter Bunny, she said, *lives in my heart.*

Then she tapped her chest, closed her eyes, and fell asleep.

∴

You gotta be fuckin' kidding me.

Thovas and I went outside and held each other, sobbing and laughing all in one. Our lifelong running joke with our mother had come to a close. That shyster, Anna. After everything, she was leaving us with a sweet little message lifted from a children's Hallmark card. The sun warmed us as we stayed that way in the shifting breeze for a while longer, lingering in the possibility that all along, Mom had been harboring this sugary truth that would stick in our teeth forever. I resigned myself to a life spent searching for meaning in Peeps, seeking truth inside a Cadbury Egg.

We wiped our eyes and returned to Anna's side to find her awake again, resurrected as it were.

She fixed me with eyes clearer than I'd ever seen and excused everyone else from the room.

I really need to talk to you, she said to me. *Pull up a chair.*

At a certain point, the dying don't want us to stop the process. They know they're dying, they're past fear. They're in control and powerful.

My mother's brain was wired from childhood to not face the things that frightened her. The personalities that stayed with Anna like angels, even as they sometimes mirrored demons, danced within her on a schedule of protection for her entire life. On the verge of death, though, every one of those personalities fled. She no longer needed them. My mother wasn't afraid for the first time in her life, and she began to speak.

I'm dying, right? she began.

Yes, Mom, I replied.

She nodded in agreement, like she'd known, but wanted to make sure before continuing.

First of all, she said, *I owe you an apology.*

Those five words had never been uttered to me by my mother before that moment. They hit me like a sack of rocks; suddenly, I was the one who couldn't absorb oxygen. For forty-five minutes straight, Anna unloaded every stone from that pile, turning it over in her hands and tossing it aside.

For years, we had no idea if Mom had been blacked out, if she was on drugs, or if she was operating as an alter. None of us ever had a clue that the horrors she'd put us through existed in her consciousness at all. She remembered every single thing: smothering me when I was three, the gerbils, the dogs, the knives, the exorcisms. The harsh words said and the loving words unsaid. She admitted to and apologized for all of it and more, things I'd always wondered about—knowings and tellings that had resulted in relationships severed, jail sentences, or worse—and explained her motives behind each action.

It all came down to darkness.

From the second I took shape in Anna's womb, my spark of light tested her. All she could do was try to snuff it out by any means she could—beat it out, suffocate it, pierce through its corona with knives and nails and words. Though it had manifested in Anna's life as a fear of the dark, what the little girl inside my mother had feared the most was *light*. Exposure. My stubborn refusal to stay down and match her darkness intimidated her. She especially hated how I gravitated toward my father's light and how, together, we'd insisted on joy as much as we could.

The one thing I could never do, she said, *is beat the love out of you. I tried. I tried to beat it out. I tried to kill it. And I'm so glad I couldn't.*

⁘

It took Mom getting to the end of her life, her mobility, and her physical beauty drained from her, for her to be vulnerable. I thought then of Margery Williams's *The Velveteen Rabbit*, one of Anna's favorites:

> Of what use was it to be loved and lose one's beauty and become Real if it all ended like this? And a tear, a real tear, trickled down his little shabby velvet nose and fell to the ground.

Like the *Velveteen Rabbit*, it was in her worn state that my mother became real. She wasn't real because the alters had left—people with DID are real and entirely valid in their own brilliant humanity. Anna was real because she realized she was free. To see the love within herself for the very first time and be able to receive love from me.

Though Mom pleaded with me to forgive her, there was nothing to forgive. I had forgiven my mother in the moment, every time she raised a hand or uttered a sharp word, every time she disappeared or shook a knife. I smoothed her hair and told her I loved her. That she had been my greatest teacher.

I meant every single fucking word. Not because I'm all enlightened, not a bit. I'd been able to forgive her because I *recognized* her. As a child, all I ever yearned for was her love. The look I had on my face when I sought my mother's eyes was mirrored precisely in the way Anna looked at *everything*. I'd known that look from the start.

I'm so proud of you, she said. *I love you. When I grow up, I wanna be just like you.*

∴

The tear that falls down the Velveteen Rabbit's face hits the ground and transforms into a fairy, who then kisses him on the nose. The rabbit's threads become sinew, and his stuffing turns to blood and guts. He is embodied, fully realized. He leaps into the air.

When I come back, Anna said next, *I'll come back as a rabbit. You'll see me in the wild, and you'll know.*

How will I know which one is you, Momma? I asked.

I'm your mother, she laughed through tears. *Of course, you'll know which rabbit I am.*

At that moment, my mother became a parent for the first time. Raising children is a course in vulnerability. We can't take care of them in the way they deserve until we can treat our inner child the way she deserved all along. We must look right into the mirror that children hold up to us and be brave enough not to look away, no matter how much that light burns.

What Anna gifted me that day was nothing short of a miracle. My mother's words were thread, silken red, mending me. My scarred skin, thick and thin, pinned to the moment with each prick of her sharp cactus needle.

She then whispered some messages to deliver to my siblings. After she finished speaking, she kissed me on the cheek.

That's all I have to say, she said.

She had made me. Then she made me real.

The last thing Anna made.

∴

Though they'd been outside, John and Thovas had gathered the clear quality of Anna's conversation. They came back into the room with eyes wide and unbelieving. Mom instantly fell back to sleep the moment we got her tucked in, stuffed animals and pillows all piled around her.

Dusk had fallen. The three of us sat vigil in Mom's candlelit room for hours, surrounding her. We spoke in quiet voices, an ear to Anna's breath.

Here and there, Ray shuffled in softly from his little room. The hospice nurse arrived, monitoring.

Sometime in the middle of the night, Thovas went home. A few hours later, John suggested I do the same. I hadn't rested or showered in days. There were rings around my eyes. There was nothing more to say, nothing more to do but wait.

The sun's first rays slowly illuminated the room. Mom looked so peaceful, resting there. Handmade eyelet embroidery surrounded Virgen de Guadalupe appliqués on pillows she had made herself. Stuffed bunnies peeked from around her frame. Glitter from the past days' crafts had settled into her skin, speckling her hair, and making her glow.

I kissed my mother on her forehead and told her I'd be right back.

Driving home through the dawn, the morning light bringing back to life the glorious miracle of a new day, I felt both at peace and exhausted. The hours, the words, had both filled me up and emptied me. At home, I sat down in the shower, curled up in a little ball as the hot water ran over me. Flecks of glitter fell from my skin, then swirled and puddled and slipped down the drain. I watched them, hypnotized. I thought of how my father had also blessed me with the same little sparks as he passed. Unlike Preston, though, Anna had left no work undone. She had completed everything she came here to do.

∴

What my mother shared with me didn't heal everything, but it filled a space with something holy. This is what rabbits symbolize to me—the nimble possibility of sudden, unexpected miracles.

Forgiveness isn't willed but waited for. Arriving only when it finds you've carved a space for it. An altar within, warm and safe, a bunny's nuzzly burrow in your heart.

Little rabbits upon my clothing promise this prospect, a wonderland dream where everything you thought impossible can surely come true, as long as you stay faithful to the hope and attentive to the wonder.

Rabbits say something about time and something about tenderness. Tenderness was hardly something I'd have ever put into the same sentence as my mother, but I'd always allowed a little space for its possibility. An Easter-morning hope, the ultimate truth—each of us deserves the possibility of redemption.

Chapter 18

LIGHT GARMENTS

FROM SITTING AT THE BEDSIDE OF SO MANY RESIDENTS AT THE retirement home, John had gathered that, often, the dying decide the exact moment to go. They can consciously release it all when the time is right.

After my shower back home, I collapsed on my bed and fell into the deepest, heaviest sleep of my whole life. About an hour into my rest, John called. Anna had passed. The drive back to her cabin crossed over the same roads, through the same scenery, but everything was different. It was now a world my mother no longer existed in.

Back in her presence, I climbed right beside my mother in her bed. I held her hands, held her face. Her eyes were closed. I kissed and kissed and kissed her mouth and cheeks a thousand times, making up for all the times I hadn't been allowed to do so while she was living.

John spoke to me. He'd been at her side, holding her hand after I left, when Anna suddenly opened her eyes and looked around the room. Her voice startled him.

John? she asked. *Am I going to go be with Preston now?*

Anna, he replied, *do you want to go be with Preston?*

Yes, she answered.

Well, then, that's where you're going, John said.

Anna had closed her eyes then, took one last big breath, and let it out. I held onto her so tightly as John told me this, tears slipping down my scarred face. I couldn't imagine anything more beautiful than that. The terror that had gripped me when my father passed, the urge to run after him into the darkness, none of these visited me that day.

∴

They say we die according to how we lived. In the end, everything caught up with Mom: emphysema, diabetes, gangrene, years of abuse, and addiction. Her passing, her process—the end, at least—both showed me an Anna I'd never met and artfully honored exactly who she'd always been.

I'd made all these beautiful dresses for my mother in those last years as her body changed. Simple shapes she could easily slip over her head, strung with ribbons, flowers, polka dots, and stars. I handled each of them that day like they were the Shroud of Turin, unfolding them gently one by one, letting the scraps of silk unfurl, ruffles and ribbons kissing the floor. Little bells I'd sewn into the hem of one tinkled sweetly as I spread the garment over my momma—each stacked upon her, layers upon layers, outfitting her for the journey. I dabbed jungle gardenia oil on her forehead and the soles of her gangrenous feet, which I then slipped into her favorite moccasins. Her rosary was already in her hand, and I stacked upon her wrists all the art metal bracelets I'd made over the years and had worn daily. John had brought some roses for Anna that he strung up and placed around her neck.

My mother never had, nor needed, a muse. She was her own—the burning core that danced amid the many personalities. Both object and subject to herself. Laying there all decked out, she looked like one of her own works of art, like the Madonnas she always painted, the dolls she stuffed and stitched together. In death, she had transformed into her own self-portrait, surreal and complete.

She glowed from within.

The corners of Anna's mouth were almost turned up in a smile. She was free from pain. She was with Preston. My mom had never been a goer, but she was happy to go this time. And she left all the baggage behind.

∴

Thovas and Amy met me at the cabin after Anna's body was taken away. Along with John, Thovas had been a witness to mine and Mom's final conversation, albeit from outside the door. If there were any hard feelings that he hadn't been the one to hear those words, he never said so. Thovas had witnessed it all. He was always the one to affirm to me, instance by instance, that what we'd suffered had actually happened. All the times I felt I could no longer trust my senses, it was Thovas who met my eyes and nodded. He was crushed. He loved Mom so much.

Anna may have tied things up with me, but I was just one fiber. Raggedy as it was, the thread of Mom's life had still kept certain things together.

Anna's death foiled Amy. It sent her into the depths, knowing she'd never have the answers to her questions. My heart broke as I listened to my sister's sobs. Her little cries had sharpened my ears for years, and I knew the sound of this one. Like from the bottom of a well. When Amy left that day, she went out and shot up heroin for the first time.

Ray said goodbye sweetly to Anna. Quietly. He spent one more night in the cabin and called me that next day, asking me to drop him off under the freeway in San Antonio. His little belongings and a few small art pieces he and Mom had made, stuffed in a duffle and signed: A.R.T.

In her last months, Ray never left Anna. Even though he was claustrophobic indoors, he hovered close. Anna had discovered him searching for treasures on the street; without her on the Earth, he had nothing anchoring him inside. I understood. All the way to San Antonio, Ray cried and cried. *Your mama was the greatest love of my life*, he just kept saying. He thought she was just so beautiful, and he'd told her so all the time, even as the teeth fell from her head and her limbs blackened. By the time I dropped him off, we were both blubbering messes.

∴

My mom will never make another thing.

I sat in Anna's room the morning she passed, looking at all the pieces she'd made in her last days. Silent gap-toothed pumpkins stared at me cockeyed, paper flowers in all stages of crinkled glittery glory. Panic sat in my throat as I surveyed that clutter my mother could never again alchemize: half-used bottles of glitter, spools of ribbon, and little pots of paint sat around her room like orphaned creatures, begging me to give them a purpose.

After my siblings came and left, and Ray went to his room, it was time for John and I to go. I grabbed a few of Anna's belongings and an old Jesus tapestry she'd kept forever that had been laid out on her dresser. It was a rendition of Leonardo da Vinci's *Last Supper*, just something she'd found at a thrift store, frayed and hand-woven like a little prayer carpet. I don't know why I grabbed the thing, but it brought me comfort to hold. I didn't let it go the whole evening, clutching it on our way home, clasping it to my chest as I fell into bed.

I couldn't sleep a wink. I shuffled with the tapestry to the kitchen, where I clicked on the bulb above our old wooden table. I sat and quietly smoothed out the fabric. As my fingertips left its texture for the first time in hours, I stood back and considered it.

Before thought, before pattern, I went through a drawer as my mother had so often before, found our heavy metal shears, and began slicing the tapestry into pieces.

∴

Before Anna had moved to the little cabin where she passed, I'd been making a kite. As a child, I constructed bedsheet kites that flew, but this one was decorative and fanciful for a friend. Even so, I hoped it would fly someday, too, and used kite string for all the stitching. The fabrics were airy but sturdy. For the kite's bones, I'd found hollow reeds around our yard. For its tail, I used ribbons of lace.

As Mom had fallen increasingly ill, the kite sat unfinished in the corner of my home, its spool of spirited thread still tethered to the last stitch. It was the only thread we had in the house—all the rest was back at Anna's cabin. I snipped it loose from the kite and found the sole needle at hand, a fat, sharp one for leatherwork.

Using these seemingly mismatched instruments was a cumbersome process. At the start, I wasn't even sure what I would make or what it would look like. I released the outcome but held fast to the thread, letting the winds of mourning direct my needle.

I'd witnessed my parents clinging to their creativity when, otherwise, their hands were empty. It's the only family crest we had; sometimes, it was the only thing we had in common. I was raised speaking the language, but I had always done so quietly, somewhat afraid of my own voice. I'd never wanted to outshine them. But now, I felt, the torch had been passed to me to keep their creativity alive.

In a torch race, preserving the sacred fire is more important than speed or competition. I didn't want to run from the pain, but I also didn't wanna stare it in the face. Not yet. It's just dumb luck that the tools available weren't a syringe or a bottle. The sadness I sat with kept me awake and pinned me to the spot like an arrow. Through this fresh wound coursed a catalyst. I had to make something even if it was for nothing.

By the morning, the piece had taken form: a little backpack, a simple drawstring with a flap.

∴

My mother was cremated a few days later, but we couldn't afford to pay for her ashes. It was a shitty feeling—like I'd left her at a pawn shop. It ate away at me every minute. I called the mortician daily to let him know I'd get the money soon and retrieve Mom.

Everything was in limbo; all I could do was wander the world with that backpack, clinging to its straps like a parachute. Trips to the grocery store were the worst—all those people who hadn't known my mother, the disorienting aisles bulging with bags of candy she couldn't eat anymore.

Excuse me, a voice startled me from my swirl. *Where did you get that bag?*

I'd forgotten that I even existed as a visible entity other people could approach, so it took me a moment to respond to her question. Plus, it felt so personal for her to ask about the backpack. I felt like I was standing there stark naked. Somehow, I managed to tell her I had made it myself, even though saying so felt somewhat untrue—the entire process had been a blur; saying I created the bag was like taking sole credit for a group project. *Would you like to sell it?* she continued.

Oh no, I answered quickly. *No.*

I couldn't believe anyone besides me could see worth in that bag, and it just meant too damn much. *It's not really that cool,* I mumbled. *It's kinda hand-stitched with kite string and whatever. It's really not that great if you look at it.* I apologized myself away and shuffled through the rest of my shopping, mystified by the whole experience—not sure if it had even happened or why. I probably would've remained in that fugue state for years if the woman hadn't popped up again in the parking lot.

John and I were slinging our groceries into the bed of the truck when she rematerialized. She told me she was sorry, but she just had to have the backpack. I stumbled over words of denial when, God as my witness, right then and there, this woman offered me the exact amount of money we needed to collect Anna's ashes.

⁖

I'd been raised to give everything away—not to be sentimental or stingy or enchanted by the world of stuff. I was ashamed of wanting to keep the bag, and I was also ashamed to sell it. I didn't feel like the thing was worth the amount of money this woman was offering. But I needed my mom's ashes, and this was just the kind of shit Mom loved. It was why she had attended to each of her saints with glasses of water, flowers and glitter and bowls of macaroni n' cheese: she believed in their intercession, in the concrete actions of angels. The laughter from Mom's cosmic *I-told-you-so* echoed as I watched this woman write out a check to me.

Backpacks symbolize the burdens we carry, but nothing was magically solved for me by selling it other than my ability to redeem my mother's remains. I wasn't suddenly unburdened, and I didn't feel any lighter. An angel, after all, isn't a savior. An angel is a messenger. The message was that there is worth in the work, the spirit of creation, and the alchemy of suffering. It wasn't gonna be an easy path or a gentle lesson. I had a long way to go.

The bag itself was crude and sutured. But it flew, after all.

I never saw that woman or heard from her again.

∴

The funeral home that held Anna's ashes was the same one my father had passed through, and it was attended to by the same man. He presented us with the identical faux-wood-paneled box that had contained my father's remains, and we drove home to release my mother at Preston's spot on the Medina River.

But the season was different. The cottonwoods on the bank were hardening into their bare, silvery winter wear. It was gray and dark and cold out, all things Anna couldn't abide. So I kept her inside.

No matter where I'd lived, I always managed to find some closet or nook to serve as my little haven, a private space where I could sit and be alone. This method had seen me through migraines, Mom's abuse, scary men, and my recovery after the dog attack. There was a teeny room next to mine and John's bedroom that I'd turned into such a place, and this is where I decided to keep Mom's ashes until spring. Though I knew being locked away in a closet was Anna's truest fear, I also knew I couldn't face that box every day.

I always kept a nightlight on for her, and she wasn't alone in there: Preston's sketchbooks sat nestled against her container. Saints, icons, and flowers kept her company. I sat and slept in there a lot over that long winter, telling Anna how much I missed her, asking how she was and if Preston was there with her. I told her stories about Thovas and Amy, about my dog Humphrey, about John, and about Jennifer Doyle.

About four months later, another fake wooden box filled with ashes joined Anna in there; Ray had never recovered from his broken heart. A routine trip to the VA hospital had gone awry, and Ray had gone to join his love.

His passing had brought another layer of grief, but it had also brought spring. Warmer weather whispered it was time to release my mother to that river, her sweet partner at her side.

∴

Mom's bean pot we'd lugged through our childhood became the proper urn for both Anna and Ray. The day was set. At the kitchen table, I married their ashes together in the bean pot urn with a hefty sprinkle of glitter and rose petals on top. The flower of forgiveness and miracles, mixed with Mom's favorite material. We surrounded the container with candles and fresh gardenia, copal incense and vials of glitter, bottles of cumin, and red, red roses. Prayer cards of Anna's beloved saints sat among the grottoes and dolls she had made, sprinkled through with pieces of hers and Ray's A.R.T. We made macaroni and cheese for her beloved Don Pedrito and enchiladas and Mexican rice for the rest of us. In the background all day played Mom's favorites: Elton John, Randy Travis, George Jones, and, of course, old Hank.

It was to be a tiny gathering, just John and me and my siblings. But by that, I mean *all* my siblings: Anna's memorial would be the first time all five of her children sat together in one room.

The two children Anna left at the orphanage before I came along had always hovered around the edges of my life. We'd never shared much time, but we shared Anna's blood—that spicy mix of searching and shaping that manifested in five totally different ways. The meeting of all my mother's children was a curious combination of sadness and relief. I thought of how my older siblings had never really known Anna, how much they must have missed her growing up, or at least the idea of her. Through stories we shared with them, Amy, Thovas, and I tried to communicate to this new contingent that it hadn't been a cakewalk. That Anna's suffering had slashed and burned whole forests of our childhood, still shy to sprout new growth.

But looking at us together, our shared features and mannerisms, I realized that our mother hadn't suffered in vain. I was in awe. Anna was a weaver, and the tapestry set before me in the faces of my family was nothing short of a masterpiece.

My mother had been on the knife-edge verge of ending my life, and her own, often. I've felt that despairing myself, the emptiness and pain that wants to lie down forever. But something had stopped her each time, saving her life and mine, even to this day. Anna had gotten us here and given each of us a chance. We had to figure most of it out on our own, but there we were, together, doing just that. For the most part, we could see the grace in it, even if it was just for a moment.

∴

Most of the letters I put on Preston's cottonwood tree had worn down to a pulp or washed away in the river, but the lump in my throat as I put my hand to its trunk still spoke. I'd clung hard to my father, releasing his ashes from grasping hands, not ready to let go. I remembered that panic, the desperation for one more conversation with him. But with Anna, I had gotten such a blessing: the opportunity to wrap up what I so desperately needed to hear in words.

The burden had been lifted from her. She was light.

And she wasn't alone—the specter of my father had ushered Anna through the process of passing, and now Ray was at her side. Their ashes floated together on the rush of the Medina in dancing swirls of oil-slick rainbow glitter. As far as the eye could see, they twinkled in the sun, spinning. When a portion got stuck in a whirl and seemed to turn back, my heart lurched. I wanted to scoop Mom up with a sieve, glitter and all, miraculously reformed into the glowing new woman I had so recently gotten to know. But as those little points of light made from the remains of my mother's earthly form reflected back to my eyes that afternoon, I understood.

I loved my mother like I love the moon—for just existing. Despite all her scars and changes, despite her cyclical darkness, she couldn't help but mirror the light of life itself.

My mom was no saint, but she'd suffered; somehow, within, she'd stayed a child. I'd had the honor of meeting that child when she spoke with me in our first and final conversation. As I watched her ashes sparkle away into the sun, what I whispered to my mother returned to my own child heart:

I love you.
I hear you.
You didn't deserve this.
I forgive you.
Thank you.

∴

I would never have a Mom to make me a pot of soup, run her fingers through my hair, and kiss me on the cheek. I would never get that particular love from my mother or father on this Earth. But I could give it.

This right there is the option that makes life interesting and beautiful. That makes it bearable. It lays the groundwork for change. It requires courage. There's so much love in the universe that belongs to us that we'll find it if we get out of our own way. It just shows up, like that woman who bought the backpack in the parking lot.

I had almost denied that messenger because I felt ashamed and afraid—historically how people react when they are confronted with divinity. Angels are terrifying because they illuminate this choice: stay small or embody all the love God keeps showing you is your birthright.

And when you choose love, watch out.

∴

No product can make you glow from within, and no potion aside from tears. Feeling the gut hurt of life and letting it roll down your face is the only way. My mother couldn't access that until the very end, but she had struggled to say it all along.

Many of Anna's dolls began on wire frames shaped like a woman's body. Gauzy layers of washed-rose fabric traced the form that hovered voluminous and expansive even for its spindly construction. Often, she would place a light inside so the entire production would radiate, warm and wondrous. She so badly wanted to feel this, but her art was the only way she could speak it.

Though she'd beaten me for decades over what I wore, she could never beat out that light inside; every single piece of clothing I've ever made has been in service to it, that brightness that burns within us no matter what—defined by the darkness that shows us, by its expansion, just how boundless the universe is. Tender and sheer, with pinholes for light, a permeable membrane of softness, that's all the armor we need to stay open to love. Never meant to cover the scars but carve star-shaped apertures for your heart to shine.

Let your wildness Ripen
as the World burns around you.
Stand in the center of that heat
until you've merged
with those flames
to help forge the way forward,
into the life you've
always imagined
the life you've truly wanted.

LAYERS AND LAYERS

THE NIGHT THE WOMAN BOUGHT THE BAG IN THE PARKING lot, and I brought Anna's ashes home, I immediately made another backpack. Same pattern, same kite string, same needle. Again, from an old tapestry, and again, it sold. Though that wasn't the goal—selling the first backpack had scared the shit out of me. It had opened a door that I wasn't ready to walk through without its secure pressure against my spine. I was disoriented without that weight. The only thing I could think to do was to make another one, strap it on my back, and continue.

I hadn't chosen my materials with any idea of sending a message—they were just what was available. Kite string brings to mind joy and lightness, but I'd been sunk like a stone when I'd threaded that fat needle. The message was sent nonetheless.

Like the letters I nailed to Preston's cottonwood tree, thread was the language I used to communicate with my mom and her saints. The kite string had lifted my broken heart up, up, up. I never expected to reel it back in and find it still beating, strong. But I needed something stronger. I wanted these bags to last.

So, I chose saddle thread. I didn't think about it. There were feed stores everywhere in Bandera, and I just picked some up one day. Waxed and heavy, but supple and cheap. Perfect. A saddle suggests a tool one needs to achieve a goal, a vehicle to the next location. The thread through my fingertips grounded me, unconsciously binding me to that intention. My work was no longer at the whim of the breezes. I'd found a scrap of confidence and brought it back down to earth. The horse—a beast of earth energy itself, a beast of prey—is an essential guide, an extension of the rider. Although I didn't have a horse, I was firmly seated atop something powerful that required me to trust it just as much. That needed me to trust God and Mary and Don Pedrito. And myself.

I wasn't there yet, but I was getting to know this beast.

∴

It isn't a given, feeling at home in your own body. These soul-suits we wear are intricate breathing machines and things of beauty. But they betray us in a million ways. Pain and panic, pathology. Perhaps others have harmed us, leaving us wandering like ghosts within ourselves.

Anna had struggled to find solace in her body, but she found beauty everywhere. She surrounded herself with reminders that life can be lovely. After she died, I took on that practice.

The house, they say, is symbolic of the womb. The first place. I'd felt so itchy in Anna's womb, ready to get out ASAP. Now, I set out to nest. Mine and John's home in Bandera was a starting-over point—a place to shed what had passed and regrow within the new mother who'd finally shown herself and inhabited me.

Layers and layers and layers of it all came to the surface. Our house became a walkable shrine to everything Anna loved. It was another way of communicating—handmade and repetitive. It poured out of me. The hallways, like my arteries, hearts and bones strewn. All the bits I couldn't yet part with and was tired of stuffing away.

The farmhouse in Forestville, California, that had been put into the care of my parents back in 1972 when I was nine years old, set the scene for my psyche. I still dream of it. And in 2002, when I was thirty-eight, I set out to recreate it. The land surrounding mine and John's home was dotted not with daffodils but wildflowers in spring. We acquired peacocks, chickens, geese, donkeys, and cows. I covered every square inch of our home with rugs, with lace, and with paint—turquoise and cobalt blue. The outdoors came inside, and the insides spilled out.

This time, no one was gonna slap a snake outta my mouth or spill all my collected rocks on the roadside. I could get it all out and bring it all in. It was chaos. Our home started as a shell, neglected and overlooked. Without setting out to do so, I nestled within those walls, feeling it all. And created a pearl.

∴

Isolated as we were out there, we still had visitors and neighbors. One woman down the road from us was a seamstress named Dixie. She'd once made purses and saddles and had all the machines in her garage ready to fire up. A friend of John's named Todd Hallmark—a free-spirit couch surfer who loved jalapeños and Red Hots—took up residence on our sofa and fronted me some money to keep the operation going. It wasn't much, but it was enough.

I still couldn't sleep and was making little things at night with my bare hands: carpet bags, waist pouches, shoulder bags, messenger bags, backpacks. All from textiles, laces, needlepoint, and tapestries and stuck with vintage brooches. These old materials inspired me; I threw myself into studying antique European bags, where no detail was spared, inside or out.

It doesn't matter if no one sees what you make, but I promise if you keep at it, people will want to. My bags had traveled through the hands of unknown strangers and fallen into the laps of angels with names. The layers of fabric, like soft armor around a raw heart, attracted the eye of other makers, who could see through. Who knew. Carol Hicks Bolton was one such seer. She sold fabrics by the pound at her antiques store in downtown Fredericksburg, and though we'd never really met, I'd always wanted to. Most of my bags were fashioned from her scraps, so I figured I'd gift her one. From that simple exchange, Magnolia Pearl stuck its foot out of the womb.

Carol carried about thirty of my bags to a furniture market, where they sold like hotcakes, and caught the eye of a woman who worked for a magazine. This woman was interested in them, interested in me, and in the home John and I were building. The day that story came out in that magazine, our phone started ringing and it hasn't stopped.

∴

When I looked at myself in my home in that magazine, all I could recognize were my father's eyes shining from within the shrine I'd built for my mother. I had a hard time seeing myself. The things I created were changing me, changing my life. It was hard to take any credit for that, and it still is. I was forced to realize that I existed and that I had a story to tell.

Not separate from my parents' legacy or the inherited signature that expressed their trauma. Not apart from them, but just a part of them. A little mirror shard of God, doing all I could to reflect the joy that bubbled up small like a river's source and rushed through my veins despite all the dams. I had been telling that story through the bags, through my home. All those textiles and paint that flooded from me then, psychedelic and electric and bold as fuck—I saw them reflected to me, and their vibration startled my senses. I didn't know why, at the time. I needed that palette to exorcize all the chaos inside, and the intention echoed with people who found inspiration in my work. It was a shock to the system. I was ready, and I wasn't.

There were times when the vibrant river dammed—where I found myself flat on the floor, skull struck with lightning bolts, buzzing and buzzing with pain that ran circles in my mind like those circus motorcycle riders in a sphere. That my migraines began to worsen just as my work was starting to flourish was no coincidence—I had fought to exist but didn't believe I deserved to shine.

∴

My mother's words to me had come just in time and healed so much, but my body hadn't caught up. Closure is never guaranteed, and healing never really happens all at once. Anna's message soothed my rational mind, but my body still believed the warnings from my animal intellect. From years of being prey, that primitive sense of perceived danger. She'd spoken the syllables to unlock the spell, but it was now on me to do the work of undoing.

Threading the eye of a needle one exhausted morning, my own eye tired. A lickety-squint moment in which I knew something had to change. I was building something; I was putting down roots, but I was still in so much visceral pain. I could honor my parents and make a home in homage, but it was time to take responsibility for myself.

The healing had to start at the scene of the crime this time—my body. My creature-self and my very vehicle for relationship and memory. Humans aren't mollusks, man. There's no hard outer shell to protect the pearl-making. It's all just soft, fragile skin. So vulnerable we all are. We gotta be so gentle with ourselves.

From the moment my mom beat me for wanting to wear little boxers instead of "girl" panties, I'd insisted upon what I put next to my skin, what clothed this container. That very dawn, I sat with thick textiles and a fat needle in my hand, and I decided to make clothes.

Of course, I'd always made them here and there. But for the first time—released by my parents' freedom and free from their judgment—I could define where they ended and where I began, at the boundary of skin that traced my being. I traded making bags for bright garments. The strings of those sacks had carried my grief and brought me to my feet; now, it was time to fly.

∴

Every single thing and being is made up of chapters—story upon story, standing on the shoulders of what came before, processing in layers: of fabric, of paint, of poetry. The very nacre of a pearl, coat by luminous coat. The old bones and spoons and artifacts within our own planet's striations. Creativity is how you both dig and soar simultaneously; the clothes I make fit both tasks.

The work only comes through the work. It requires absolutely everything of you, and the only real and lasting return of any of it is your self, realized. Who you've always been beneath. Released in the layers: rising, rising.

Still, shit returns—that Levite-hem tug back to the foot of the Ferris wheel. It feels sometimes that life is a string of events that happen to you; after a few rounds, you realize that instead, it's something you live within, move within, and shape from within. You're handed a spool of thread and asked what you can make of it all. Not to shed the layers but incorporate them, piece by raggedy piece, beloved and perfect as is.

POSTSCRIPT

"It is a little stardust caught, a little segment of the rainbow which I have clutched."

—HENRY DAVID THOREAU

THAT MAGNOLIA PEARL WOULD BE CONSIDERED A "SUCCESS" in the eyes of the world was never something I expected or even dreamed of. My aims were always shaped like those shops that raised me, shot through with murals and soaring messengers—a saint in every corner and stars everywhere: Banana Funk N' Junk, The Refinery, The Little Grotto Shop. They were often the most stable spaces in my life, where my mother floated in her only safety, and my father fostered connection. They were never anything grand but were always ground zero for creative people in the community—the ones who never felt entirely understood or seen. My father wove service into each storefront, and even Anna couldn't help but feed others from the Grotto Shop she built out of sheer soul survival. It was in that shop that she began to heal, even as her physical health took a nosedive.

Success doesn't look like what we think.

Magnolia Pearl clothing can be found in hundreds of boutiques across the globe and is worn by people I've watched on movie screens or listened to sing my heart whole. We've got two storefronts, one in Fredericksburg, Texas, and another in Malibu, California. By all accounts, this is the definition of success, and you better believe I'm grateful for every bit of all it's built. But my idea of success is something much smaller and much bigger—something that shares and shifts, something unfinished and constant.

Success isn't an endpoint.

The Bible verse that says "to whom much is given, much will be required" is usually understood as a statement on wealth, that people with more are meant to share it with those with less. And I believe this to be 100 percent true, but that's just one part of it. Because it was the times when my hands were empty that I realized the actual responsibility this verse implies: whatever it is we're blessed with, we're meant to shine it from our hearts and share it to the benefit of others. This is success in action, that heals both the giver and the recipient. It's a success that doesn't hoard but releases and returns ten-fold.

Writing this book has been an exercise in healing, and that healing is the true success. But like success, healing is also something forever unfinished and fluid. Magnolia Pearl's clothes mirror this quality—always a little raw, a little undone, and light. A love for the process you can see and feel and wear.

Having been hungry, it's always been my prayer to feed people. My mom's bean pot was one of the only materials I inherited from my parents, a literal and ethereal symbol. It was often the only possession we had, the one we'd lug around the neighborhood—the vessel my mother fed strangers from and held the ashes of her final form. For all that had been taken from Anna, she healed only when she gave to others from the wealth of her heart. This wasn't just a success, but a triumph. I honor it the very best I can.

Magnolia Pearl is a vessel dressed. Our aim is to inspire and reflect inspiration and reverberate hope in magical and practical ways. Through the Magnolia Pearl Peace Warrior Foundation, we seek to nourish, educate, and provide aid to vulnerable populations around the world. Each dream nurtured is sustenance. Each full belly is the greatest success. From there, so much is possible, I promise.

To learn more about Magnolia Pearl and the Magnolia Pearl Peace Warrior Foundation, please visit www.magnoliapearl.com.

YOU'LL NEVER UNDERSTAND THAT LIFE IS A PLAY ON WORDS, BECAUSE YOU'LL NEVER BE ALONE ENOUGH TO REFUSE HATE, JUDGEMENTS, AND EVERYTHING THAT NEEDS A GREAT EFFORT, IN FAVOR OF AN EVEN, CALM STATE OF MIND IN WHICH EVERYTHING IS EQUAL AND UNIMPORTANT.

TRISTAN TZARA ON DADA

Preston's journal

In the time of your life, live—so that in that good time there shall be no ugliness or death for yourself or for any life your life touches. Seek goodness everywhere, and when it is found, bring it out of its hiding place and let it be free and unashamed.

Place in matter and in flesh the least of the values, for these are the things that hold death and must pass away. Discover in all things that which shines and is beyond corruption. Encourage virtue in whatever heart it may have been driven into secrecy and sorrow by the shame and terror of the world. Ignore the obvious, for it is unworthy of the clear eye and the kindly heart.

Be the inferior of no man, or of any men be superior. Remember that every man is a variation of yourself. No man's guilt is not yours, nor is any man's innocence a thing apart. Despise evil and ungodliness, but not men of ungodliness or evil. These, understand. Have no shame in being kindly and gentle but if the time comes in the time of your life to kill, kill and have no regret.

In the time of your life, live—so that in that wondrous time you shall not add to the misery and sorrow of the world, but shall smile to the infinite delight and mystery of it.

—WILLIAM SAROYAN, *THE TIME OF YOUR LIFE*

Acknowledgments:

Thank you, PAIN, for teaching me to listen.

Thank you, PAST, for guiding me to forgive.
Thank you, grief, for reminding me I'm still breathing.
And thank you, breath, for the opportunity to live.
Bring roses to the places and pieces
you struggle to love within your
own heart. See those spaces
in others, and fill them with
Compassion.

We are here to take care of one another.
What a gift to bear witness.

Thank you, God, for dreaming me.
And thank you, Reader, for joining me.
Together, let's pay it forward.

Forgiveness
is Everything

ABOUT THE AUTHORS

ROBIN BROWN is a tightrope artist, fire-juggler, certified clown, and ringleader. She's magic, but she'd be the last to say so. She'd rather see the magic in you and not rest until you see it, too.

She's got forty-four bobby pins in her hair, ribbons tied to her wrists, and a tick-tock locket in her chest that's right on time. At home barefoot in the sun, listening to someone—really listening—and telling them what they're feeling is okay. To love anyway.

She lives the spirit of the first law of thermodynamics, which states that matter is neither created nor destroyed but transformed. She's a telescopic kaleidoscope, seeing through gravity to point out colorful shards of light. She's a human, a creature. In awe.

Forever bewildered.

JESS BRASHER is a poet, memoirist, and mother.

She would like to dedicate her work to Rex Brasher, with deepest gratitude to Robert, Candace, and Hannah.

Printed in the USA
CPSIA information can be obtained
at www.ICGtesting.com
JSHW011902030624
64252JS00002B/2

9 798989 722251